Job Description Manual for Medical Practices

3rd edition

Job Description Manual
for Medical Practices

3rd edition

Courtney Price
PhD

Alys Novak
MBA

Medical Group Management Association© **(MGMA©)** publications are intended to provide current and accurate information and are designed to assist readers in becoming more familiar with the subject matter covered. Such publications are distributed with the understanding that MGMA does not render any legal, accounting, or other professional advice that may be construed as specifically applicable to an individual situation. No representations or warranties are made concerning the application of legal or other principles discussed by the authors to any specific factual situation, nor is any prediction made concerning how any particular judge, government official, or other person will interpret or apply such principles. Specific factual situations should be discussed with professional advisors.

Production Credits
Editorial Director: Marilee E. Aust
Project Editor: Anne Serrano, MA
Composition: Virginia Howe, McIntire Publishing Services
Copy Editor: Mary Kay Kozyra, Valley Editorial Services
Proofreader: Kelli Davis
Indexer: Lucie Haskins
Cover Design: Ian Serff, Serff Creative Group, Inc.

MGMA Information Center Subcommittee
Chair: Charles D. Moses, FACMPE
Samantha Kempster, MBA, CMPE
Carolyn Pickles, MBA, FACMPE
Mary Pat Whaley, FACMPE

Library of Congress Cataloging-in-Publication Data
Price, Courtney H.
  Job description manual for medical practices / Courtney Price, Alys Novak. -- 3rd ed.
    p. ; cm.
  Includes index.
  Summary: "The third edition of Job description manual for medical practices continues the MGMA tradition of providing human resource management publications that serve as classic references for medical practices. These 100 job descriptions are divided into three major categories: business, clinical, and specialty, and then subdivided by key departments"--provided by publisher.
  ISBN 978-1-56829-279-3
1. Medical personnel--Job descriptions--Handbooks, manuals, etc. 2. Health facilities--Employees--Job descriptions--Handbooks, manuals, etc. I. Novak, Alys. II. Medical Group Management Association. III. Title.
  [DNLM: 1. Job Description--Handbooks. 2. Health Personnel--Handbooks. 3. Practice Management, Medical--Handbooks. W 49 P945j 2008]
  RA971.35.P75 2008
  610.69--dc22
                              2007040808

Item #6660
ISBN: 978-1-56829-279-3

Printed in the United States of America
10 9 8 7 6 5 4 3

Contents

Preface

The third edition of *Job Description Manual for Medical Practices* continues the MGMA tradition of providing human resource management publications that serve as classic references for medical practices.

In 1991, the first edition of the manual was written at the request of MGMA members who wanted a set of generic examples to use as the basis for creating their own job descriptions or to check against existing descriptions. The book became a standard resource for medical practice administrators. As one reader said, "Job descriptions were not plentiful when I started working in physician offices. In one office, we had to write our own job descriptions. We struggled as we made them up or tried to find them elsewhere. If we had been fortunate enough to have owned a copy of the manual, it would have made our jobs so much easier. What a great resource for physicians and medical practices, hospitals, home health, adult care facilities, research centers, laboratories, and emergency care clinics."

The second edition, published in 1999, addressed three key factors: new legislation, such as the Americans with Disabilities Act, which made it imperative for job descriptions to become more focused on specifics; technology, which changed so many jobs in so many ways; and major driving forces, such as quality improvement, risk management, utilization management, and outcomes research, which created many new jobs.

These factors are still in play and even stronger today. As the world changes, so do jobs and job descriptions. The result: Publication of the third edition reflects the needs of health care in the new millennium and the effects on the top 100 medical practice jobs.

These 100 job descriptions are divided into three major categories: business, clinical, and specialty, and then subdivided by key departments. Some medical practices will need few descriptions; some will need more; and some will need unique ones. The top 100 jobs described in this manual represent the most typical.

Acknowledgments

The authors applaud the continued support from MGMA over the many years they have produced human resource management publications for its members. Particular thanks go to Marilee Aust, Publisher, Knowledge Management and Information Center, who helped to produce the first edition of this manual 16 years ago. We are grateful for her ongoing support of this project. We also thank Marti Cox, Knowledge Management Manager, for digging into the databases and linking us to key resources that were pivotal during the updating process.

Special thanks go to Susanna M. Hancock, AAS, RMA,CMA, RPT, COLT, and an American Medical Technologists board director, who not only reviewed the prior edition and suggested specific updates but also shared specific job descriptions related to her areas of expertise. Her time and talent were invaluable to the project.

In addition, we thank Greg Rossman, Chief Human Resources Officer at Denver Health and Hospital Authority, who provided us with valuable information that made the job descriptions cutting-edge. Many thanks also go to Richard Hansen, MD, and Lance Goudzwaard, CEO of Arapahoe Gastroenterology, PC, for providing us with an invaluable group practice perspective.

We also thank Jill Hansen, MBA, for her help in formatting and creating the forms. We are grateful for all her help in putting this together.

NOTE: Because this manual is designed for a national audience, the authors and MGMA cannot ensure that the manual adheres to the legal requirements of each locality or state. Rather, an attempt has been made to consider the impact of federal law and nationwide legal trends. Consult your legal counsel about your specific employment policies to ensure that they follow the legal requirements in your locality and state.

CHAPTER 1

Introduction

"Job," as defined in *Random House Webster's College Dictionary* (Random House, 1995), is a "piece of work, especially a specific task done as part of the routine of one's occupation or for an agreed price." It is also defined as "a post of employment; position." Other defining words: project, responsibility, duty, performance, a unit of work. In short, job descriptions define the work of particular kinds of jobholders so they know what they are supposed to do.

These definitions have remained relatively stable over the years, but the work world and its jobs have not. The world changes, work changes, jobs change. As social, technological, economic, and political changes occur, the jobs that need to be done, how jobs are done, who performs specific jobs, when and where jobs are done, and, most important, why jobs are done evolves as well. The obvious example: Technological advances such as the development of the computer and its various applications, including the Internet, have profoundly changed not only how work is done but also what must be done. Technology has been, is, and will be a colossal force in the work world far into the future—when artificial intelligence programs and robots are likely to take over many jobs.

In the United States, robots already perform some health care functions, such as helping to fill prescriptions. In Japan, robots serve as caregiving "companions" to the elderly. Artificial intelligence (AI) computer programs that use computer "eyes" for the visually impaired are being developed in many countries. Computerized prosthetics speed the recovery of paraplegics. Even low-tech applications are increasing, particularly those for service animals that sense epileptic seizures or smell out cancer and monkeys that are trained to be the "hands" for the disabled. Whether high tech or low tech, these changes are affecting job descriptions. For example, just about every job description in this manual reflects that computer skills are required.

Technology: The Number-One Impact

Technology is neutral. However, the way it is used can create both positive and negative results. For medical group practices, administrative use of a computer for maintaining electronic medical records, diagnosing medical conditions, and using the Internet to transmit patient health, billing, and other information to others has significantly increased efficiency. It has also opened the door to possible theft of such information. Congressional concern about patient privacy and confidentiality resulted in the Health Insurance Portability and Accountability Act (HIPAA), which requires major changes in medical practice systems.

One result: Existing jobs were "tagged" to reflect who has the need to know certain information about patients, and new jobs and job descriptions were invented to handle related new functions, such as HIPAA compliance. These regulations affect every job description. In this manual, confidentiality is noted in almost every job description along with infection control, safety, and quality assurance requirements. They are now standard elements of medical practice jobs.

Confidentiality is a key part of the trend of e-mail and Internet penetrating medical practices. Not only does staff communicate electronically more frequently with each other and the external world, but so does the public with the practice. It's increasingly common to build a Website with information about the medical practice and to post patient education items, job openings, special events, new service offerings, and other information. It's also fairly common today for practices to encourage patients to electronically refill prescriptions, get information about health conditions, make appointments, get test results, and "talk" to their physician.

This type of communication has its own challenges. Physicians may be concerned about how much to share electronically. Is it appropriate to provide information without being able to look into the patient's eyes and ask enough questions to ensure the person understands the information? Obviously new protocols are necessary—protocols that facilitate communication in the best possible way. What type of information, for example, should a medical assistant, RN, nurse practitioner, or physician assistant convey instead of a physician? How will this affect their job descriptions? These are all questions to be answered.

Follow the Trend: Update Your Job Descriptions

The realities of today's workplace mean not only new types of jobs and integrating technological applications into existing jobs. They also mean dealing with social trends such as diversity in terms of patients and staff. A job description for a receptionist, billing specialist, or other positions may need to be rewritten to state that fluency in a particular language (being bilingual) is a requirement. It also may mean outsourcing interpretation/translation jobs to contractors who should perform in accordance with the medical practice's job descriptions. Outsourcing a variety of jobs from billing to information technology (IT) to collection to translation offers some cost efficiencies but it also brings specific management challenges. Specific job descriptions can help communicate effectively with contractors.

Economic trends, often triggered by political trends such as consumer and politician outcries about health care costs, may continue to force changes in Medicare reimbursement. This, in turn, can trigger cost-cutting measures by medical practice administrators, including changes to existing jobs. Medical practices may make budgetary moves to combine jobs, increase job-sharing, outsource, multitask, eliminate jobs, and switch tasks from physicians to nonphysician positions. On the other hand, economic growth may generate the need for a satellite office in a newly developed area, which in turn creates the need for more jobs. Each type of restructuring should automatically trigger a review of current job descriptions and development of new ones. Managers must ensure that continual updating occurs to keep staff and the organization on track with today's realities and trends.

Customization of Job Descriptions

As you modify job descriptions, ensure they fit your medical practice. Do you have a small practice? Then you may need descriptions that "bundle" many job functions. Your few support staff may multitask automatically, e.g., answer the phones, make appointments, greet patients, and handle insurance authorization and billing. Do you have a large practice? The volume of patients requires several staff members to do the same job. For example, you probably have many staff members who handle only billing. Is your practice located in a rural area? You may need to consider job-sharing because of a labor shortage in your community. Are you in an urban area? You may need to add a bilingual requirement to some job descriptions. Are you outsourcing some functions? These "staff" also must comply with your job descriptions. Are you a single-specialty practice or multispecialty? An academic practice? Are you a nonprofit? Do you use volunteers?

All of these factors mean that generic job descriptions, as presented in this manual, are only a starting point. Use these descriptions as the foundation for a standard job and then adjust them to fit your situation. (More details on how to do this are included in a later chapter and also on the CD-ROM that accompanies this manual.)

As in any other field, new ideas about how job descriptions should be written keep popping up. Some recent ideas suggest including:

- job competency information that meets the mandate of the Joint Commission (on the Accreditation of Healthcare Organizations) to assess, prove, track, and improve the competence of all employees. Most job description developers tend to provide competency information specific to jobs as separate documents rather than integrate it into descriptions.
- skill-based descriptions that emphasize the knowledge, skills, and abilities of a specific person. The intent is to encourage employees to build their knowledge, skills, and abilities so they become more valuable to the organization and to themselves. This approach may be particularly useful in small medical practices that promote cross-training and multitasking.
- employee-written descriptions that allow employees to design their own jobs and identify their own accountabilities in terms of performance, productivity, and outcomes. This technique promotes a sense of freedom for the employee, but it can also complicate the organizational structure, particularly the compensation system.

- brief job descriptions that seek to capture a job in a few sentences (a very small "sandbox") to allow for considerable freedom outside the box. As with employee-written descriptions, these tend to be more confusing than liberating. Also, they often do not meet legal requirements for being specific about essential functions, work environment, and physical/mental demands.
- flexibility that is better expressed as "keeping up with the times." As noted, updating descriptions should be a continuous improvement effort. As supervisors and employees see a job changing, they should work together with a human resource (HR) specialist to flexibly move the job into reality.

The point: The basic job description, as presented in this manual, will continue to be a vital tool for both employers and employees. Regardless of what happens in the future, the benefits of having job descriptions include:

- providing a record of continuous improvement over time;
- helping management with HR planning, recruiting, and staffing;
- facilitating continuity as the practice evolves;
- supporting managers if they must defend their personnel decisions because of grievances and/or litigation;
- communicating expectations effectively when outsourcing jobs;
- minimizing the chaos of not knowing who does what and ensuring workload inequalities do not occur; and
- helping modify old assignments and create new ones.

Job description methodology will continue to evolve. It continues to be the safest way for employers to have documentation that supports employment decisions and avoid legal issues and complications related to hiring, training, and terminating staff. Most important, its main purpose remains stable: to clearly communicate what the organization wishes to achieve and how the employee helps fulfill those goals.

CHAPTER 2

Overview

Medical practice managers must make successful hiring decisions based on clear, current information about what tasks must be performed to achieve the organization's goals and what qualifications are required for these tasks. Managers also must know how to clearly communicate job expectations and requirements to new employees and updated job requirements to current employees. It is also important to know how to tie these expectations and requirements into performance evaluations. Managers must understand the requirements of a job before promoting or terminating an employee. A well-written, accurate, complete, and current job description helps fulfill these human resource (HR) responsibilities.

This manual helps you as a medical practice manager to fulfill your responsibilities. This section clarifies:

- who should use the *Job Description Manual for Medical Practices*;
- what the manual includes;
- when to use the manual; and
- how job descriptions serve multiple purposes.

Who Should Use This Manual

This manual is designed for anyone in a health care organization who manages staff and is responsible for some HR tasks. In medical practices, that person may be the supervisor along with the office manager, the business administrator, and the HR specialist—whoever is responsible for ensuring the organization has the right staff to perform the proper tasks in the most appropriate way.

The manual will assist recruiters, interviewers, trainers, compensation managers, HR planners, legal/compliance coordinators, researchers, supervisors, managers, and physician owners. It will assist senior executives who own and operate the practice to develop strategic plans and measure employee performance. Effective job descriptions will help them focus on the organization's mission, hire effective team members, develop career ladders, and establish management succession plans.

The manual also is designed to be used by employees. Employees should understand how an organization designs and analyzes jobs, develops job descriptions, and uses job descriptions as a major HR management tool. Thus, the manual should be used as a communication vehicle with new employees and referred to when critical HR steps are taken, such as performance evaluations, professional development, or job description updating. The more employees understand and respect the job description process, the more likely they will understand how—and why—the organization manages its human resources the way it does.

Most important, when employees understand the why, what, and how of their job descriptions, their job performance and professional development should improve. There will be little room for misunderstandings about what is required, what to do, and why it is important. The supervisor and employee should have many opportunities and occasions to communicate about job descriptions and related performance standards. Employees should be able to discuss various aspects of their job descriptions with their supervisors and suggest changes and innovations. Therefore, the manual should always be available as a resource for all staff members. In addition, take these two positive steps. First, place all job descriptions in a binder and place the binder in a central location such as the HR specialist's office. Also, post all job descriptions on your Website for review by interested potential and existing employees.

What the Manual Includes

The manual describes the:

- critical steps to take as you develop and maintain job descriptions;
- legal requirements affecting job descriptions;
- options to consider if you want to expand the utilization of job descriptions;
- strategies for implementation and updating job descriptions; and
- trends related to job descriptions that medical practices may wish to incorporate into their HR policies.

When to Use This Manual

You will want to use this manual to:

- develop job descriptions;
- update job descriptions;
- comply with legal requirements;
- clarify job descriptions for content and format;
- understand the multipurpose role of job descriptions;

- improve employee performance; and
- manage HR functions more effectively.

How Job Descriptions Serve Multiple Purposes

Because jobs are continuously changing, the importance of up-to-date job descriptions increases. It is critical to remember that these documents have multiple purposes; they should be the vehicle for the 10 key HR management functions outlined in the flowchart.

JOB DESCRIPTIONS
VERSATILE MANAGEMENT TOOL

1 Strategic Planning
- Conduct SWOT analysis.
- Develop operational plan.
- Define future direction and growth.

2 Management
- Implement strategic plan.
- Analyze and plan organizational systems and structure.
- Identify staffing needs.
- Design jobs and work flow.

3 Compensation
- Set salary (salary surveys).
- Determine salary increases.
- Establish recognition and rewards.

4 Hiring
- Recruit.
- Screen applicants.
- Describe job.
- Interview.
- Review qualifications.
- Select.

5 Orientation
- Introduce:
  - medical practice
  - goals
  - culture
  - policies and procedures

6 Supervision
- Explain:
  - organizational fit
  - reporting relationships
- Provide training and development.
- Offer coaching.
- Review disiplinary procedures.
- Review termination policies and processes.

7 Retention
- Reduce turnover.
- Improve employee morale.

8 Promotion
- Identify career opportunities.
- Create career ladders.
- Promote as develop.

9 Safety Matters
- Describe:
  - working conditions
  - physical demands
- Identify hazards.

10 Legal Issues
Comply with:
- ADA
- Title VII
- FLSA
- Equal Pay Act
- EEO
- HIPAA, etc.

Strategic Planning

Job descriptions should first be used at the strategic planning stage when your medical practice makes plans for its future direction and growth; this typically occurs annually. The senior managers developing the plan will consider the medical practice's current strengths, weaknesses, opportunities, and threats (SWOT). For example, a practice has an opportunity to build on its pediatric specialty. However, it faces the threat of a shortage of pediatric RNs in the marketplace. What's the solution? Or consider the advent of "convenience clinics" at local drug stores. Planners could look at this trend and ask themselves several questions: Why does this new service appeal to consumers? Is this a threat to our primary care operations? These clinics are staffed by physician assistants and nurse practitioners, have lower prices, and offer quick in/out service. Is there an opportunity for the medical practice to do something similar? How would such a service impact job descriptions?

It is important to note that senior managers will also explore the social, technological, economic, and political trends on the horizon that are most likely to impact the medical practice. For example, the world is moving rapidly toward Internet/e-mail communication with patients. How will the practice take advantage of this trend? It is also a fact that American citizens are aging. How can the practice best offer geriatric care?

Managers must evaluate these issues when considering what jobs need to change to meet new realities, what new jobs need to be added, and what existing jobs may need to be eliminated. Consider how personnel planning will be affected by a decision to add a specialty, develop a satellite office, upgrade technology, merge with another practice, or move responsibilities from physicians to nonphysician providers. The outcome of strategic planning typically is a series of departmental operational plans for each business and clinical unit.

Management

After the strategic plan has been finalized, the person responsible for HR functions should help each department manager build a staffing plan by using the job description as the primary tool for any planned restructuring. As the strategic plan is implemented, any needed additions or revisions to job descriptions are triggered as the department managers plan and adjust operations to match the new direction.

This operational planning/analysis often triggers a new look at work flow, work load, and job design. This type of management task is done at the macro level, rather than at the individual level. It's a useful exercise to involve several layers of management or key decision makers at this stage to get a big-picture perspective of how work might be done to best meet the practice's future needs.

Compensation

The job description is the cornerstone of the compensation process and determines internal job worth—how valuable a job is to the medical practice. As a first step toward developing a salary schedule/pay plan, those who decide how to compensate employees must determine what jobs are "worth" to the organization. This is done using external salary surveys to identify the market value of the job and then set the salary scale for each job. The job description provides the necessary data for this step and helps management defend its pay decisions in employment disputes.

Job descriptions also help managers decide how to reward employees as they progress in performance and proficiency and meet targeted goals. They are also used to identify the compensation path as employees change jobs and continue up the career ladder. The salary range for each job identifies pay increases as an employee develops professionally. The knowledge, skills, and abilities noted in the job description are "values" that measure worth.

Hiring

In the first phase of the hiring stage, the job description is used to instruct the recruiter on how to write a job posting and search for those who can fulfill the job requirements, that is, it specifies the target for the recruiter. The most critical step in the hiring process is to review job descriptions and develop job search criteria before advertising a job opening. It is important to know what you want before you go looking for it in potential candidates.

In the second phase, the job description helps the hiring manager or the HR specialist screen resumes and application forms. By comparing the job description qualifications with the applicant's profile, the screener can usually eliminate 80 percent of the candidates and invite 20 percent for an interview.

After several candidates have been recruited and screened, the interviewer uses the job description to more carefully focus on the match between the needs of the job and the person's qualifications as specified in the document. The interviewer can also use the job description as a "talking tool" to describe the job during the interview. It is appropriate to share the job description with applicants and get their thoughts about the closeness of the match.

After reviewing everyone's qualifications against the job description measuring stick, the hiring manager/supervisor will feel more confident with his or her final selection.

Orientation

After a candidate has been selected and hired, the job description is used to highlight the medical practice's goals, its policies and procedures, and its culture. The job description is then used continually as supervisors and other staff train new employees in precise tasks and explain how the job fits into the organizational structure and mission.

Supervision

After orientation, the supervisor uses the job description to explain how a new employee's job fits into the organization. The description also clarifies reporting relationships (who is your boss) and any supervisory responsibilities of the employee (who do you boss). Considerable time should be spent identifying how the job description specifies expected performance and thus links to performance evaluation. Think of a job description and a performance evaluation as "bookends" that directly correlate in terms of initially explaining what is expected in terms of performance and then identifying whether expectations have been met.

Communication with the employee about performance standards to be met as he or she performs the essential job responsibilities begins at orientation and continues every day as the supervisor reinforces what is to be done, how it is to be done—and why it is to be done via a performance plan. Discussions about performance should never be a once-a-year event. They are part of the continuous improvement and professional development process, probably the most important process within the medical practice. This type of constant surveillance of performance allows supervisors to efficiently identify performance problems, correct them, and terminate an employee if necessary after being given an opportunity to improve.

The sample performance evaluation form on pages 11–13 is designed to complement a job description so employees recognize the direct link. Note that the form begins by spotlighting the essential job responsibilities and the performance requirements related to knowledge, skills, and abilities. Ideally, the form is used as a performance planning tool. It can be used during orientation to collaborate on a three-month plan for expected performance and then updated at each review. By the time of the annual review, there should be no surprises because the job description and the performance evaluation form have shown the way to success from start to finish.

PERFORMANCE EVALUATION FORM

Employee_____ Title _____

Department_____Supervisor_____Date _____

Purpose of evaluation: ☐ 3-month ☐ 6-month ☐ Annual ☐ Other

Instructions: This form should be used to (a) develop a performance plan for the employee and (b) to track/evaluate performance. Responsibilities, goals, and priorities should be mutually agreed upon by the supervisor and employee. Accomplishments should be noted prior to the performance review by the employee and then discussed with the supervisor during the review to ascertain that performance expectations were met.

Essential Job Responsibilities: (List the 3–4 major responsibilities.)

_____

_____

_____

Performance Goals: (List 3–4 goals related to these responsibilities that are tied directly to organizational goals, e.g., quality patient care, excellent customer service.)

_____

_____

_____

Professional Development Goals: (List goals related to the knowledge, skills, and abilities needed for this job.)

_____

_____

_____

Accomplishments: (Provide specific evidence of achievement related to each type of goal. *This section is filled out by the employee prior to review with supervisor.*)

_____

_____

_____

Supervisor's Evaluation: (Indicate the supervisor's assessment of performance related to each goal using this scale.)

1	2	3	4
Does not meet goal	**Meets goal**	**Above goal**	**Exceeds goal**

(Continued on next page)

General Performance Factors: (Indicate supervisor's assessment related to employee's performance behaviors by circling the rating using the same scale. The supervisor should support the rating with a comment about a specific observation[s] of the behavior.)

Initiative: Sees beyond the immediate assignment and acts on opportunities/problems.

        1   2   3   4

Observations:

_____

_____

Follow-through: Sees that objectives and related action steps are taken to completion.

        1   2   3   4

Observations:

_____

_____

Interpersonal Relations: Listens carefully, presents self and one's ideas effectively.

        1   2   3   4

Observations:

_____

_____

Teamwork: Works effectively with others to achieve group goals.

        1   2   3   4

Observations:

_____

_____

Patient Relations: Displays respect, patience, helpfulness to patients in friendly manner.

        1   2   3   4

Observations:

_____

_____

Overall Performance Summary:

        1   2   3   4

Comments:

_____

_____

Development Planning:

Employee strengths to develop further:

_____

_____

_____

_____

Knowledge, skills, abilities to improve:

_____

_____

_____

_____

Goals for next period related to responsibilities:

_____

_____

_____

_____

Action Plan:

_____

_____

_____

_____

Next Review Date:_____

Supervisor's Signature:_____**Date:** _____

Employee's Signature:_____**Date:** _____

(Acknowledges employee has reviewed and discussed evaluation.)

Retention

The job description is an indispensable tool to make sure employees not only perform to expectations but are motivated to stay with your medical practice. By letting staff know they are on the mark and recognizing their contributions, employees will remain with the organization and keep producing and developing. The result: reduced turnover, which is costly to any organization.

Retention is achieved one employee at a time; however, feeling "like I fit" is personalized and the cumulative effect of each satisfied, motivated employee is huge. A low turnover rate results in improved employee morale across the board. It is also a neon light that attracts new employees who want to fit too because "this must be a good place to work."

Promotion

One major way to bolster retention is to ensure that employees are aware of career growth opportunities within the organization. Create career ladders and have them available so employees know there is a logical upward path. One example: A certified nurse assistant could aspire to become a licensed practical nurse and to move on and become a registered nurse by acquiring the appropriate training and education. Job descriptions for these positions make it clear what qualifications are needed to move up. Then, if he or she chooses, can work toward gaining the necessary knowledge, skills, and abilities.

An employee who is promoted is, in effect, a "new" employee for that particular job. Therefore, orientation, training, and performance standard clarification must be conducted again, using the job description as the communication and measurement tool.

Safety Matters

Each job description should describe the work environment in terms of the conditions and the physical demands the jobholder will encounter. Is the employee exposed to communicable diseases and/or biohazards? Is he or she exposed to radiation? The job description also should note the kind of physical activity involved—walking, standing, bending, twisting, reaching—or if it primarily is a sedentary job.

This level of detail in a job description identifies working conditions that could endanger the health of an employee. This information assists in helping the organization comply with the Occupational Safety and Health Act (OSHA), which is a major legal requirement.

Legal Issues

Job descriptions should not only provide information to guide the work of specific jobholders, they should also contain global information that covers all employees. This information not only specifies safety considerations (e.g., working conditions such as the level of hazard) but also reflects legal requirements. One key example is that job descriptions must comply with the Americans with Disabilities Act (ADA) by concentrating on essential job responsibilities (i.e., the key functions the jobholder must be able to perform). For instance, a computer helpdesk job description might specify that the person must be able to answer technical questions via phone and e-mail but no heavy lifting of computer equipment is required. A disabled person who uses a wheelchair would be able to do this job with perhaps some reasonable accommodations, e.g., adjustment of the desk and use of a headset.

Here are the major employment laws that affect job descriptions:

The **Americans with Disabilities Act of 1990 (ADA)** prohibits private employers, state and local governments, employment agencies, and labor unions from discriminating against qualified individuals with disabilities in job application procedures, hiring, firing, advancement, compensation, job training, and other aspects of employment. The ADA covers employers with 15 or more employees. Not every disabled person is protected by the Act. The person also must be qualified, i.e., an individual who, with or without reasonable accommodation, can perform the essential functions of the job in question. The job description must clearly define those essential job responsibilities, the work environment, the equipment operated, the physical demands, as well as the required knowledge, skills, and abilities. Any person can then be compared with this job profile to ensure the qualification standard is met. Your HR specialist has the expertise to ensure that you comply with this critical legal regulation.

The **Equal Employment Opportunity Act of 1972**, referred to as EEO, extends the anti-discrimination provisions of Title VII of the 1964 Civil Rights Act. Your lawyer and HR specialist will help ensure that your job descriptions, hiring, and other employment practices comply with the mandate that individuals must be protected against employment discrimination on the basis of race, color, gender, national origin, and religion. It applies to employers with 15 or more employees. There are two other legal issues to consider related to EEO. When writing job descriptions, list only the minimum necessary requirements such as education and experience. It is acceptable to note preferred or desirable additional factors, but the emphasis must be on only those that are necessary to ensure members of minority groups are not artificially screened out. Also, job descriptions should not state that a job can only be performed by a licensed professional when that is not actually a requirement of the state. For example, states require that RNs be licensed; however, medical assistants are not required to be licensed.

The **Equal Pay Act of 1963 (EPA)** covers all employers who are covered by the federal wage and hour law under the Fair Labor Standards Act. It requires that men and women be given equal pay for equal work in the same establishment. The job content, as described in the job description, determines whether jobs are substantially equal.

The **Fair Labor Standards Act of 1938 (FLSA)**, as amended, established minimum wages, equal pay, and overtime; outlawed child labor; and specified record-keeping affecting most full- and part-time employees. One critical part of the law spotlighted in job descriptions is the designation of "exempt" or "nonexempt" job classifications. Exempt means that employees holding these jobs are not eligible for overtime pay. These are primarily professional positions. For example, if registered by the state, nurses meet the learned professional exemption and may be classified as exempt if paid on a salary basis of at least $455 per week. Nonexempt employees, such as clerks, are eligible for overtime in the event that they work more than 12 hours in a work day or if they work more than 40 hours in a work week. The Department of Labor designates which jobs are in which category and the designations do change occasionally. Supervisors should work with the HR specialist to make sure they know which positions are exempt or nonexempt and what that means in terms of overtime pay and other factors.

The **Health Insurance Portability and Accountability Act of 1996 (HIPAA)** not only focuses on accountability for ensuring patient privacy and confidentiality, it also protects the portability of health insurance benefits if an employee changes or loses his or her job. Although job descriptions do not need to specify the "need-to-know" level of a job, they frequently emphasize the confidentiality requirement. In all cases, it is important for the supervisor to clearly define a job's confidentiality factors. For example, a clinician caring for a patient needs to know the person's diagnosis; a janitor in the facility does not.

The **Occupational Safety and Health Act of 1970 (OSHA)** established regulations to provide for the health and safety of employees on the job. The Act aims to ensure better working conditions by working with employers and employees on work environment conditions. The section in a job description titled "work environment" is a response to this Act and must consider such environmental factors as lighting, work space, and possible hazards. Employers must identify, track, and report occupational injury and illness trends. Every medical practice should have a safety training plan and conduct such training during orientation and at regular times during employment. Examples of training include courses on body mechanics, infection control, and biohazard protection.

There are many other legal requirements that affect dealings with employees and have an indirect relationship to job descriptions. One example is the Family and Medical Leave Act (FMLA). If an employee develops a serious health condition, his or her ability to continue working on either a full- or part-time basis should be compared with the job description. Work with your HR specialist to learn how employment laws interact with job descriptions, from recruiting at the beginning of the cycle to termination at the end of the relationship.

Internal Revenue Service

The Internal Revenue Service (IRS) requires employers to classify their employees as either independent contractors or employees. If your medical practice contracts with health care workers, such as medical transcriptionists or interpreters, there are many requirements to be met. The IRS will look closely at how a job is fulfilled by an individual to ensure that the organization–individual relationship is truly "independent."

Joint Commission

Collaborate with your clinical services, quality improvement, and human resource managers on meeting Joint Commission (formerly the Joint Commission on the Accreditation of Healthcare Organizations [JCAHO]) standards relating to job descriptions. These are not legal requirements; rather they are vital guidelines to follow to ensure quality patient care. The Joint Commission suggests that health care employers develop written job descriptions for all job categories and all units as a way to define job expectations and evaluate job performance. The Commission suggests that job descriptions outline job responsibilities, minimum education, and other requirements, such as licensure for the position and degree of supervision received or provided by the position. It specifically recommends that job descriptions address infection control responsibilities, safety responsibilities including exposure to hazardous materials, and activities unique to the work setting of the position. As previously mentioned, information about expected competencies also must be available.

CHAPTER 3

The Job Description

What Is a Job Description?

The most common term for the document that spells out the responsibilities and qualifications related to a job is *job description*. However, you may also run into two other terms: position description and job specification.

A *position description* describes the work done by one individual and may or may not be identical to a job description. An easy way to think of a position description is to remember that only one person can occupy a position at one time. Another way to differentiate the two definitions is to think of the job description as describing a job in general and the position description as describing a job as tailored for or by one specific individual. When employees are asked to write their own job descriptions, in effect, they write position descriptions because they describe their jobs in an individualistic manner.

Supervisors sometimes modify a generic job description to fit the work and qualifications of a specific individual who is hired for a job. For example, suppose a person hired for a position has a different but related skill than the one noted in the job description or has additional skills not noted. Or suppose the person hired to be a Medicare biller also knows how to bill Medicaid. The job description becomes a position description when this task is added to the job responsibilities listed. Generic job descriptions also may be modified into position descriptions when an organization restructures. Consider a medical practice that decides to outsource its translation/interpretation needs rather than hire bilingual staff. The practice adds this contractor coordination task to its health educator job responsibilities.

A *job specification* is a written description of the job responsibilities of a job class (a group of positions with similar responsibilities) so that the same title may be used, the same salary may be equitably applied, and the same qualifications required. For example, there may be a claims/billing processor group of jobs with all the jobholders doing basically the same job but handling the claims of different payers. A job specification is quite extensive and is the result of a thorough job analysis (described later in this chapter).

In this manual, the term *job description* is used because it is a common, readily understood term. However, the job description format shown in the manual is comparable to a job specification in that it provides extensive information about the context of each job.

What Is Included in a Job Description?

Many types of information can be included in a job description. Some types are considered standard and others considered optional. This manual spotlights standard items. However, as you customize these descriptions, feel free to add the optional items listed at the end of this section or others that fit your needs. The standard items include the following:

Job Title: The job description begins by naming the job, e.g., registered nurse, medical transcriptionist, chief technology officer. It briefly and specifically defines the key facts of the job. Anyone having this title should perform the same set of duties and thus have the same purpose throughout your medical practice. Note that a job title may not necessarily mean the same thing in another organization.

Department: Job candidates and jobholders need to know the department in which they will work. For example, a registered nurse may work in the pediatric department, the geriatric department, or another department performing general nursing tasks.

Immediate Supervisor Title: Every job candidate and jobholder needs to know about the reporting relationship, i.e., who is the boss.

Job Supervisory Responsibilities: Some jobholders are also supervisors. An RN may supervise LPNs and/or CNAs. An executive assistant may supervise an administrative assistant.

General Summary: This section serves as the synopsis of the job. The key facets of the job in terms of the type of work performed are presented in a couple of sentences. This thumbnail sketch is often used in recruitment advertisements and career development information. It also typically includes information about whether this job is classified as exempt or nonexempt.

Essential Job Responsibilities: The heart of the job description, this section spotlights the essential functions critical or fundamental to performance of the job. For example, an accounting manager's essential job responsibilities would include assisting in preparing various financial and statistical reports, overseeing preparation and accuracy of monthly financial statements, and communicating financial information to management.

In some instances, "givens" such as "complying with patient confidentiality, infection control, and safety regulations" are included in this section and/or emphasized in the performance requirements (knowledge, skills, and abilities) section. However, these givens are also conveyed as HR policies and may not be included in job descriptions. Just make sure they are covered in any discussion of the job with applicants and emphasized during orientation as well as during ongoing supervision.

Because jobs do change, supervisors may need to have jobholders do more or different tasks. To provide flexibility in the job description, the list of essential job responsibilities can conclude with a general statement such as "other duties as assigned" or "other responsibilities as needs occur." The following language can be placed at the end of each description: "This description is intended to provide only basic guidelines for meeting job requirements. Responsibilities, knowledge, skills, abilities, and working conditions may change as needs evolve." This type of statement also should be spotlighted in the employee handbook.

Education: List formal education required (level or degree of study) or the equivalent. For example, "RN degree from an accredited school of nursing." As noted in the previous discussion on legal factors to consider, specify the minimum necessary requirements to ensure against discrimination. It is acceptable to note preferences, e.g., "BSN preferred."

Experience: List type and amount of experience required; specify the minimum necessary. For example, "minimum of three years experience as receptionist in a health care setting, preferably in a medical practice."

Other Requirements: In this section you note other necessary requirements related to formal credentials, licensure, or certification—for example, current state RN license. You may also note a current cardiopulmonary resuscitation (CPR) certificate for clinical positions.

Performance Requirements: The knowledge, skills, and abilities necessary for the job are highlighted in this area of the job description. *Knowledge* is defined as the information a person must have acquired through education and experience. Knowledge is the prerequisite for the thinking and action required to fulfill tasks. Knowledge can be verified by tests such as school exams. For example, a Medicare billing clerk must know about Medicare regulations and claims processing. *Skills* refer to demonstrated proficiency/competency when performing a task, i.e., showing that you have the knowledge and know how to use it. An example is a Medicare billing clerk who correctly files a Medicare claim. *Abilities* refer to the innate capacities a person is born with that are needed to perform required tasks proficiently. There are mental capacities (e.g., verbal, mathematical, spatial intelligence) and physical capacities (e.g., visual acuity, hand–eye coordination, agility, range of motion). As an example, an accounting jobholder needs to have the capacity to perform mathematical calculations.

Equipment Operated: List the equipment necessary to perform essential job responsibilities. For example, most employees in today's medical practice need to operate a computer and use specific software programs.

Work Environment: In this section you describe the working conditions related to the job. Note elements such as dirt, dust, smoke, fumes, temperature, lighting, toxic substances, and exposure to biohazards and communicable diseases. For example, an RN working as a dialysis nurse will have more environmental exposures than a triage nurse who primarily deals with patients by phone.

Mental/Physical Requirements: List the physical demands of the job, e.g., walking, sitting, standing, lifting, bending, stooping, reaching, twisting. This description of physical and mental exertions relates to mobility, weight-lifting, visual requirements, patient care handling, and dexterity level and should also note the level of emotional stress, such as dealing with emergencies.

To ensure you are clear about these requirements for ADA (see the legal discussion) and other purposes, be specific to the work that will be performed in your clinic when you describe physical and mental demands and the work environment. For example, specify what percentage of a work day that a task or condition is performed, e.g., 80 percent of the day is spent standing. It is important to specify weight-lifting requirements, etc. (Note: The generic job descriptions in this manual do not attempt to be specific because demands and conditions vary. Be sure to modify and/or expand to fit your situation. If several jobs have the same type of physical and/or mental demands, this information could be noted on a separate sheet rather than in the job description.)

Optional Items: You have the option of including other items for specific job descriptions. For example, descriptions for senior management positions often include additional accountability factors to consider. These might include:

- *Interpersonal relationships involved.* This is particularly important when the jobholder must interact with a wide range of audiences or specific critical audiences such as people of different ethnicities/nationalities, payer representatives, or government regulators.
- *Impact of error.* Some jobholders must perform tasks where an error will have significant impact. For example, a key computer department employee may inadvertently cause the computer system to crash with a ripple effect across the medical practice.
- *Degree of difficulty.* Some jobs or tasks are more difficult than others, and this should be noted. For example, a receptionist answering calls from those who speak another language may only need to have a conversational level of language fluency. However, a bilingual nurse may need a clinical level of language fluency or use an interpreter competent to communicate clinical details.
- *Level of access to confidential data.* Some job descriptions identify the level of "need to know"; however, this information may be provided in a variety of formats, such as during orientation. As noted previously, those providing patient care need to know the patient's diagnosis, whereas the janitor does not.
- *Degree of independent judgment.* Senior managers often must make significant judgments by themselves or only in consultation with others. They need to be able to do this quickly, just as senior clinicians occasionally need to decide quickly, by themselves, about a patient's care.
- *Critical success factors.* Some medical practices specify the "biggies" in their job descriptions—the two to three critical factors that determine success when per-

forming the job. As an example, the chief financial officer's success rests on the ability to maintain the medical practice's financial stability. This may be stated in the job description and will likely be a hot topic of discussion when the chief financial officer meets with the chief executive officer about performance expectations.

- *Competency*. As previously noted, to meet Joint Commission requirements, it is important to identify the competencies jobholders must have. Usually this information is presented separately from the job description. You might consider including a generic statement, such as "The jobholder must demonstrate current competencies applicable to the job."

- *Salary range*. Some job descriptions, as well as job postings, provide compensation information. This information also can be provided separate from the job description.

What Does a Job Description Look Like?

The sample job description form that follows illustrates the format just described. You can use it as is or modify it to fit your needs. The generic job descriptions presented in this manual follow this format.

JOB DESCRIPTION FORM

Job Title: _____

Department:_____

Immediate Supervisor Title:_____

Job Supervisory Responsibilities: (List numbers and titles.)

_____

_____

General Summary: (Summarize purpose of the job and note exempt/nonexempt status.)

_____

_____

_____

_____

Essential Job Responsibilities: (List four to six essential responsibilities/functions; end with "other duties as assigned.")

_____

_____

_____

_____

Education: (List formal education/degree required or equivalent.)

_____

_____

_____

_____

Experience: (List type of experience and minimum years of experience required.)

_____

_____

_____

_____

Other Requirements: (List any necessary licenses, certifications, etc.)

_____

_____

_____

Performance Requirements:

    Knowledge: (Note knowledge required for tasks whether acquired through education or experience.)

_____

_____

_____

    Skills: (Note required level of demonstrated proficiency/competency for performing specific tasks.)

_____

_____

_____

    Abilities: (Note innate capacities needed to perform required tasks proficiently, both mental abilities, e.g., verbal, mathematical, spatial intelligence, and physical abilities such as, visual acuity, hand-eye coordination, agility.)

_____

_____

_____

_____

Equipment Operated: (List equipment necessary to perform essential job responsibilities and skill level needed.)

_____

_____

_____

Work Environment: (Describe the environmental conditions where essential job responsibilities are performed, e.g., setting, air quality, temperature, noise, biohazard exposure.)

_____

_____

_____

(Continued on next page)

Physical/Mental Requirements: (List the physical demands of the job with percentages, e.g., walking, sitting, standing, lifting, bending, stooping, reaching, twisting, and mental demands such as frequent emergencies, demanding deadlines.)

_____

_____

_____

_____

Optional: (List additional factors to consider, especially for executive positions.)

- Interpersonal Relationships Involved
- Impact of Error
- Degree of Difficulty
- Level of Access to Confidential Data (e.g., patient, financial, administrative)
- Degree of Independent Judgment (e.g., planning, decision making)
- Critical Success Factors
- Other

_____

_____

_____

_____

What Are the Steps Involved in Developing a Job Description?

Techniques for developing job descriptions are used to help managers meet legal requirements and other compliance needs, hire the right people, evaluate performance, compensate, and terminate. Before developing job descriptions, the steps described in the following paragraphs need to be taken.

Job Analysis

A job analysis is the first step in the job description process. It involves observing and identifying job content by studying the various facets of a job, such as physical requirements, work environment, knowledge, skills, abilities, and responsibilities required of the worker in terms of activities and qualifications. The end result is a job description that includes the type of information presented in the job description form.

Participants in the job analysis process include the job incumbent/the person who presently holds the job; the supervisor who manages the jobholder and is responsible for his/her performance; and a HR specialist or job analyst/consultant who has been trained in these techniques. A previous jobholder might also be involved. A useful way to discover what the current job entails is to have an employee who is being promoted or is leaving the company provide information about the job.

These people perform three tasks:

1. Identify the job in terms of its purpose, i.e., how it contributes to the achievement of the organization's mission. Be sure to differentiate this job from all other jobs in the medical practice.
2. Describe the job tasks, reporting relationships, physical and mental demands, and work environment. Be specific about what the jobholder does.
3. Specify the qualifications for successful job performance, i.e., what knowledge, skills, and abilities it takes to do this job well.

The development of a job description is a work in progress. Updating should be constant and job analysis should be done continuously; i.e., it should be a regularly scheduled event in the life of a medical practice. Ideally, job descriptions should be updated annually. This is crucial. Managers who review employees infrequently face considerable danger. Outdated descriptions trigger turnover, perpetuate unsafe conditions, and foster unrealities and counterproductive performance expectations. Try this insurance step: Ask employees to update their own job descriptions once a year and share their thoughts with their supervisors. This will inspire a useful discussion and perhaps prompt a new job analysis.

To be more specific about timing, there are several key moments, other than the annual review, when you need to develop or review job descriptions. These include:

- new job creation;
- restructuring the practice;
- technological changes;
- new procedures/methods;
- frequent job turnover;
- compensation changes;

- expanded duties for certain jobs; and
- job tasks shifted to other jobs.

There are four common ways to perform a job analysis. These are: the interview, the questionnaire, the observation, and the diary/time log. These can be used alone or in combination.

Interview

The interview is conducted by a job analyst or HR professional who is a trained interviewer. He or she uses a prepared script or questionnaire to gather information from the present or past jobholder and the supervisor on such topics as essential job functions, reporting relationships, and work environment. The interview is done in a conversational manner with emphasis on putting the jobholder at ease. This method also provides the flexibility to deviate from the "script" if interview answers give new insights and suggest a new direction. As with all the methods, this method has advantages and disadvantages.

Advantages

- An interview is most likely to gain the cooperation of the interviewees because of the personal approach.
- A script and tape recorder eliminates the need for the interviewee to do a lot of writing.
- The interviewer is able to gather complete information through repeated, probing questioning.
- It can be done with a group; the analyst can interview several employees with the same job at the same time.
- It leads to standardized information gathering, which increases consistency.
- It allows the interviewer to get a strong sense of the critical elements of the job after interviewing several incumbents about the job.

Disadvantages

- This method takes lots of time if numerous jobs are being analyzed.
- The time involved may preclude interviewing everyone.
- The method is expensive; time equals money.
- It requires a skilled, trained interviewer.

Questions typically asked in a job analysis interview can be as simple as:

- What is the title of your job?
- What do you do in a typical day, in sequence?
- How much time does each task take?
- What is/are the most important task(s)? Why?
- What do you need to know, be skilled at, and be able to do?
- Why is your job important? What purpose does it serve?

- Who supervises you? Whom do you supervise?
- What equipment do you use?
- What are the working conditions? Are they hazardous?
- What has changed about your job since the job description was developed or revised?

Other useful questions are:

- How and when are you evaluated?
- How satisfactory is the supervision you receive in terms of helping you do your job well?
- What other resources might you need to do your job better?
- What tasks are you doing that you should not be doing?
- What tasks are you not doing that you should be doing?

Job incumbents are the job experts, and both their factual information and opinions are valid in terms of providing insights into the "real" job, not the one on paper.

Questionnaire

The questionnaire is the most commonly used job analysis technique because it is usually quick and easy to conduct. There are many job analysis questionnaires available, all with advantages and disadvantages.

Advantages

- The questionnaire is an economical method; it is the least costly.
- The method allows information about many jobs to be gathered rapidly and at one time.
- It can be used with many employees.
- An employee can complete a questionnaire in a short time.
- It is easy to tally and analyze and it is easy to report the data.
- The method can be used without much training.

Disadvantages

- It is difficult to find or develop a questionnaire that fits all jobs.
- It limits off-the-subject information.
- It may confuse some employees, and their answers may not be clear or consistent.
- The questionnaire may not be returned by all employees.
- The method may encourage group answers rather than individual ones.

The job analysis questionnaire (pages 28–29) can be used with any job and by any employee to gather general information. Supervisors and HR specialists can also use the questionnaire to provide information for the job description (page 30). In addition, supervisors can use the supervisor input needed for developing/updating job description questionnaire to trigger their thoughts.

JOB ANALYSIS QUESTIONNAIRE

Person Completing Form _____

(Name and Title)

Date of Completion _____

Job Title _____

Department _____

Immediate Supervisor Title _____

Job Supervisory Responsibilities (numbers and titles)

_____

_____

_____

Essential Job Responsibilities

_____

_____

_____

Education Required

_____

_____

_____

_____

Experience Required/Preferred

_____

_____

_____

Any Other Requirements (licenses, certifications, etc.)

_____

_____

_____

_____

Knowledge Required

_____
_____
_____

Skills Required

_____
_____
_____

Abilities Required

_____
_____
_____

Equipment Operated

_____
_____
_____

Work Environment

_____
_____
_____

Physical/Mental Requirements

_____
_____
_____
_____

Optional (other information)

_____
_____
_____

SUPERVISOR INPUT NEEDED FOR DEVELOPING/UPDATING JOB DESCRIPTION

Supervisor Name: _____ Date: _____

Others Providing Input: (Include names and titles, e.g., department manager, HR specialist.)

_____

_____

1. What minimum knowledge of specific subjects usually learned in school or prior job experience is essential to perform this job? What skills and abilities are needed?

2. What job tasks, if any, require previous experience before an employee can begin doing this job? Are there any special requirements such as licensing?

3. What job tasks, if any, require on-the-job training when the employee starts the job? What is the estimated length of time to learn each task?

4. What kinds of instructions (verbal or written) are provided for this job? How are they delivered (materials, demonstrations, one-on-one coaching, classes, video/audio, online)?

5. If job requires independent judgment or planning, give examples of decisions required and guidance provided.

6. Are regular supervisory duties required of position holder? If so, list job titles, number of employees in each category, and nature and frequency of such supervision.

7. Is contact with others required? If so, identify types of necessary interpersonal relationships, purpose of internal/external contacts and frequency.

8. Does job require working with confidential data? If so, describe the nature of the data, degree of confidentiality/need-to-know, and effect of inappropriate disclosure.

9. Note job tasks where errors have significant impact. Describe effect and how damaging it could be in terms of delays, costs, or medical practice embarrassment.

10. Describe the physical demands (e.g., standing, walking, lifting, reaching, stooping, pushing) required to perform the work and how often required. Describe the mental demands (e.g., dealing with emergencies or patients with life-threatening conditions).

11. Describe the working conditions and the setting in which the work is performed. Note any potential accident or health hazards related to the work, even though all possible safeguards are observed.

12. Other comments.

Observation

The observation method is often used when employees are unable to take time for interviews or questionnaires. It is also useful when the job analyst wants to confirm information gained through the other two methods. Of course, there are advantages and disadvantages to this method.

Advantages

- The observation method is most useful when combined with another method as a way to clarify and verify information.
- The analyst sees the reality of the job and does not rely on information gained through other methods.
- It can help resolve any differences that may exist between the information provided by jobholders and the information provided by supervisors.
- Employees and supervisors do not have to spend time writing or being interviewed because the job analyst records information in writing or via an audio- or videotape recorder.
- It provides accurate information if conducted by a trained observer.

Disadvantages

- Observation requires a trained observer who has enough experience with the jobs to understand what he or she is seeing.
- Because the method is time-consuming, it cannot be used for all jobs.
- It requires watching more than one employee with the same job to ensure that accurate and complete information is obtained.
- Jobs that take a long time to complete and those involving mostly mental activity are difficult to observe.

Diary/Time Log

This method can be used in a variety of situations. For example, it is often used in service industries such as a law firm to identify how much time is spent performing certain tasks such as advising a specific client. It can be used to tally how often a task is done during a day or week as well as how long a task takes to perform. Managers can use this appropriately as a time-management tool for themselves. The advantages and disadvantages to this method are outlined here.

Advantages

- This method is useful for capturing how workers actually use their time.
- It can provide useful insights about job functions that take more or less time than expected.
- It can identify legitimate tasks that do not show up on the job description such as taking the time to "chat" with patients to ease their anxiety.

Disadvantages

- Employees may be annoyed about having to stop and fill out a log.
- It may lead to employees "inventing" data.

- The log method may not generate adequate data because of poor or incomplete response.
- It may lead to inconsistent data.

Writing a Job Description

Once you have gathered information about a job by one or more methods, it is time to create a document that clearly, completely, and accurately conveys relevant information to the job incumbent, his or her supervisor, potential job candidates, and those involved in HR functions.

Before beginning, consider these things to do and things not to do.

Things to Do When Writing a Job Description

1. Focus on job content—what the job is really about, not extraneous information.
2. List only necessary requirements. You can focus on specific expectations when the employee has mastered the essential job functions.
3. Keep education and experience job-related. This is critical for regulatory reasons but also ensures the jobholder has the background to succeed in the position.
4. Describe fully the physical and mental requirements and work environment.
5. Keep records of job analysis information. You will want to refer to this information when you begin your next revision cycle or in the case of an EEO action.
6. Build flexibility into the job description. Provide the foundation for a true position description tailored to fit the job incumbent's specific knowledge, skills, and abilities.
7. Allow room for growth and development by turning the job description into a personalized position description that has room for increased responsibility.
8. Make sure job descriptions focus on results, making it clear what outcomes are expected.

Things Not to Do When Writing a Job Description

1. Do not contaminate the job description by concentrating on the job incumbent. The job analysis and job description must focus on the job, not the person.
2. Do not confuse desirable requirements with necessary requirements. It is acceptable to mention what is preferred or desirable only after emphasizing the minimum necessary requirements.
3. Do not use potentially discriminatory methods or terminology. Avoid possible discrimination with wording that adversely affects someone in terms of race, age, gender, handicap, veteran status, or religion.
4. Do not be vague. Be as specific and clear as possible.
5. Do not detail every activity of the jobholder. A job description spotlights the essential job responsibilities.
6. Do not make the job description long. Use an outline format as a way to keep it brief.

7. Do not use the phrase "other duties as assigned" as the summary statement at the end of the essential job responsibilities section without noting in the employee handbook or elsewhere the fact that "responsibilities, knowledge, skills, abilities, and work environment may change as needs evolve."

Tips to Consider When Writing Job Descriptions

To ensure that job descriptions are as specific and clear as possible, it is useful to follow these guidelines:

- Rank-order essential job responsibilities. Put the most important first, followed by those that are less important. Include occasional duties at the end so the employee is clear about priorities.

- Provide time data if possible, such as "This task should consume about 15 percent of the day/week or total workload."

- Develop a pie chart of job duties showing priority duties, with the amount of time allocated for each. The total should add up to 100 percent. Include room for the occasional duties. For example, 10 percent of time is allocated for extra, unspecified duties. You will find that this graphic, when used as an attachment, will imprint key messages of the job description better than words.

- Provide an organizational chart that shows how the position fits into the "big picture." This graphic also helps imprint the reporting structure, interpersonal relationships, and the overall structure of the organization.

- Use action verbs when writing responsibility statements. The job description should "show" the job in action, i.e., an employee should be able to "see" what the job entails and how it is performed.

- Avoid sexist language by using neutral/genderless words or plurals. Do not specifically infer that certain jobs are "male" or "female" jobs, e.g., do not discuss a nurse's job in female terms only.

- Use quantitative words as frequently as possible, e.g., "must occasionally lift up to 50 pounds."

- Avoid ambiguous words or phrases. Rather than saying "does filing," say "sets up and maintains files according to medical practice standards on a daily basis."

- Avoid brand names unless they are critical to the description. Say "photocopying," not "Xeroxing."

- Limit the use of the word "may." Use more specific language, such as "periodically will substitute for the receptionist" rather than "may substitute."

Tips for Implementing Job Descriptions

If your medical practice has never had formal job descriptions or a system for performing job analyses and writing specific descriptions as presented in this manual, your first step is to determine if you want to do this and, if so, why, how, when, and who will tackle the job. Put together a task force to help you identify the following:

- What the practice hopes to accomplish through the use of formal job descriptions.

- Who will participate in the process, for example, HR specialist and a selection of managers, supervisors, and employees.

- What steps will be taken and on what time frame.
- Who will write the descriptions and who will perform the reviews.
- How will the job descriptions be "rolled out" into the medical practice.
- How will updating of descriptions be ensured.

These decisions and this planning should occur at the senior-management level with input from human resources and legal counsel. A single person should have the title of project manager and be responsible for carrying out the project on time and according to plan. Involve employee representatives from departments throughout the practice to make sure you get broad input and buy-in.

You may find it helpful to use a master job description template, such as the one provided in this manual, to serve as the model for departments when writing job descriptions. This will add consistency and ensure that information is gathered for all key elements. Ask each department project coordinator to have his or her job description writers check for:

- accuracy,
- completeness,
- objectivity,
- currency,
- consistency,
- standardization, and
- clarity.

Set a deadline for when drafts must be turned in to the project manager and have them reviewed by two or three people who have knowledge of the job. When the content is satisfactory to this group, send the drafts to a designated person who will edit the copy for grammar and style. These drafts then go to a senior management group for review, modification as needed, and approval. Finally, have legal counsel check to make sure the descriptions comply with legal requirements.

After this final review, it's time to roll out the job descriptions via announcements from the chief executive officer and the project manager. The announcement should not be a surprise because you have communicated about the project from its start and many employees have been part of the process. Meet with all department managers prior to the roll-out and provide brief training on how to introduce the job descriptions to their teams. This is a perfect time for supervisors to meet one-on-one with each of their employees to go over the description together, discuss any questions, and reinforce performance expectations.

Make all job descriptions available in a binder located in the HR department or where other personnel information is kept. Also, post the job descriptions on your intranet site for easy access. You can also post the general summary of the job descriptions on your Internet site to provide general information about your practice. Be sure these are posted when you have job openings.

Once the job descriptions are published, it is time to establish an updating plan. This plan should also be used when job descriptions are already in place. The plan should include a strategy for routine, timely review of job descriptions as well as performing reviews whenever it is necessary. As noted previously, as a rule of thumb, every description should be reviewed annually by the supervisor, jobholder, and a HR specialist and appropriate changes made.

A natural time to do this is during the annual performance evaluation. This type of updating helps to focus the evaluation meeting and provides an effective outline for discussions about future performance expectations. To start the process, give the employee a copy of the current job description and ask him or her to review it and come to the meeting with recommendations for change. Supervisors, of course, should review their own job descriptions regularly and discuss them with their managers as well.

In addition, whenever there is a significant event, such as restructuring, reorganization, or introduction of new technology, job descriptions should be reviewed to ensure that they are still appropriate. New descriptions may need to be developed. Keep in mind that it may be apparent when a specific job description should be updated; however, it is easy to forget that this change may ripple across other jobs. Be sure to take a look at all related jobs as well.

CHAPTER 4

Summary—Into the Future

As stated in the first chapter, the world keeps changing, jobs keep changing—and so must job descriptions. Yes, the basic components of the job of registered nurse or accounting manager may remain fairly constant over time. However, all medical practice jobs will continually be subject to change because of the opportunities and threats affecting the organization, as well as the social, technological, economic, and political trends that never stop influencing the health care field.

Too often, job descriptions are either not created or are rarely reviewed and updated. Consequently, employees and their jobs "wander off" in directions that differ from what was originally intended and in ways that may not be realized by the supervisor, department manager, or senior management—and may not be appropriate. Ask your HR specialist to trigger an annual review as a minimum requirement and to remind you when a change in the practice may also indicate it's time to review one or more jobs.

As you move into the future with your job descriptions, remember they are the blueprints that keep all employees operating within the realm of their responsibilities. They help employees effectively plan and manage their time and operate as a team. Most important, job descriptions help the medical practice achieve its goals.

Also, remember to maximize job descriptions! It's a multipurpose tool that can help you in many ways. It helps you communicate job responsibilities and expectations starting at the selection process through orientation, training, supervision, evaluation, discipline (and termination, if necessary), and development and promotion.

The job description can be a medical practice's most effective HR tool. Use it well—in all its roles!

CHAPTER 5

Top 100 Job Descriptions for Medical Practices

Introduction

Following are the top 100 job descriptions for medical practices. They are divided into three categories—business, clinical, and specialty—and subdivided into departmental categories. The list is not all-encompassing. Some medical practices will have other types of jobs; these 100 job descriptions are the most common jobs in most medical practices.

Whether you have a small medical practice and only have 15 to 20 job categories or a large practice with 100+ jobs, use these generic examples to get a head start on developing and reviewing your own job descriptions. Customize them to fit your own unique situation; have them checked by legal counsel—and put them to work!

BUSINESS JOB DESCRIPTIONS

ADMINISTRATION

- Administrative Assistant
- Administrator
- Business Office Manager
- Chief Executive Officer
- Chief Operating Officer
- Compliance Officer
- Executive Assistant
- Facilities Manager
- Office Manager
- Receptionist
- Satellite Operations Supervisor

Administrative Assistant

Job Title:	Administrative Assistant
Department:	Administration
Immediate Supervisor Title:	Office Manager, Business Office Manager, Chief Operating Officer, Facilities Manager, or Satellite Operations Supervisor
Job Supervisory Responsibilities:	None
General Summary:	A nonexempt, position responsible for assisting supervisor with daily activities and projects.

Essential Job Responsibilities:

1. Monitors the current status of the work for supervisor.

2. Maintains supervisor's travel arrangements and appointment calendar. Arranges appointments, meetings, and conferences. Contacts the appropriate persons to attend.

3. Attends meetings or conferences as assigned and reports on major points and actions resolved or to be taken.

4. Handles variety of matters involving contact with various staff, board members, medical committees, government agencies, and the public.

5. Composes correspondence and disseminates to appropriate individuals. Answers phones.

6. Prepares various documents and handles confidential matters in accordance with clinic rules and procedures.

7. Other duties as assigned.

Education:	High school diploma or equivalent. Some college preferred.
Experience:	Minimum two years of administrative experience, including one year with a health care organization.
Other Requirements:	None

Performance Requirements: *Knowledge:*

1. Knowledge of organizational policies, procedures, and systems.
2. Knowledge of office management techniques and practices.
3. Knowledge of computer systems, programs, and applications.
4. Knowledge of research methods and procedures sufficient to compile data and prepare reports.
5. Knowledge of grammar, spelling, and punctuation.
6. Knowledge of purchasing, budgeting, and inventory control.

Skills:

1. Skill in taking and transcribing dictation and in the operation of office equipment.

Abilities:

1. Ability to establish and maintain effective working relationships with other employees and the public.
2. Ability to work under pressure, communicate and present information.
3. Ability to read, interpret, and apply clinic policies and procedures.
4. Ability to identify problems, recommend solutions, organize and analyze information.
5. Ability to establish priorities and coordinate work activities.

Equipment Operated: Standard office equipment including computers, fax machines, copiers, printers, telephones, etc.

Work Environment: Position is in a well-lighted office environment. Occasional evening and weekend work.

Mental/Physical Requirements: Involves sitting approximately 90 percent of the day, walking or standing the remainder.

Administrator

Job Title:	Administrator
Department:	Administration
Immediate Supervisor Title:	Chief Executive Officer, Board of Directors
Job Supervisory Responsibilities:	Managers and directors of all departments
General Summary:	An exempt, management position responsible for leading and directing operations in smaller organizations. Responsible for assisting the chief executive officer in leading and directing operations in larger organizations.
Essential Job Responsibilities:	1. Manages the daily operation of the organization by creating and implementing policies and procedures. 2. Directs operation of the organization and supervises all staff. 3. Helps chief executive officer develop organizational strategic plans and objectives based upon identified needs of patients.
Education:	Master's degree in health care administration, business administration, or health administration.
Experience:	Minimum seven years executive-level experience including five years of experience in the administration of a health care organization.
Other Requirements:	Licensure or ability to obtain licensure when background credentials warrant.

Performance Requirements: *Knowledge*

1. Knowledge of principles and practices of health care planning and management sufficient to manage, direct, and coordinate the operation of a health care organization.

2. Knowledge of the purposes, organization, and policies of the community's health systems sufficient to interact with other health care providers.

3. Knowledge of the policies and procedures of a clinic sufficient to direct its operations and to provide effective patient care.

Skills

1. Skill in exercising a high degree of initiative, judgment, discretion, and decision-making to achieve organizational objectives.

2. Skill in analyzing situations accurately and taking effective action.

3. Skill in establishing and maintaining effective working relationships with employees, policy-making bodies, third-party payers, patients, and the public.

4. Skill in organizing work, making assignments, and achieving goals and objectives.

5. Skill in exercising judgment and discretion in developing, applying, interpreting, and coordinating departmental policies and procedures.

Abilities

1. Ability to assume responsibility and exercise authority over assigned work functions.

2. Ability to establish and maintain quality control standards.

3. Ability to organize and integrate organizational priorities and deadlines.

Equipment Operated: Standard office equipment including computers, fax machines, copiers, printers, telephones, etc.

Work Environment: Position is in a well-lighted office environment. Occasional evening and weekend work.

Mental/Physical Requirements: Involves sitting approximately 90 percent of the day, walking or standing the remainder.

Business Office Manager

Job Title:	Business Office Manager
Department:	Administration
Immediate Supervisor Title:	Chief Financial Officer
Job Supervisory Responsibilities:	General supervision over business office staff
General Summary:	An exempt, management position responsible for directing and coordinating the overall functions of the business office to ensure maximization of cash flow while improving patient, physician, and other customer relations.

Essential Job Responsibilities:

1. Plans and directs registration, patient insurance, billing and collections, and data processing to ensure accurate patient billing and efficient account collection.

2. Manages the business office within the established budget, including annual planning, and develops monthly status reports.

3. Reviews current status of patient accounts to identify and resolve billing and processing problems in a timely manner.

4. Establishes and implements a system for the collection of delinquent accounts ensuring third-party payers are contacted.

5. Establishes and recommends credit and collection policies. Makes recommendations for improvement.

6. Maintains contacts with medical records and other departments to obtain and analyze additional patient information to document and process billings.

7. Develops and oversees business systems and works with information technology to ensure timely and accurate implementation.

Education:	Bachelor's degree, preferably in business administration or related field.
Experience:	Minimum five years of experience in a medical business office, two years as a department manager in business office department.
Other Requirements:	None

Performance Requirements: *Knowledge:*

1. Knowledge of business management and basic accounting principles to direct the business office.

2. Sufficient knowledge of policies and procedures to accurately answer questions from internal and external customers.

3. Broad-based knowledge of relevant insurance regulations and familiarity with the Health Insurance Portability and Accountability Act.

Skills:

1. Skill in establishing and maintaining effective working relationships with other employees, patients, organizations, and the public.

2. Skill in developing, implementing, and administering budgets.

Abilities:

1. Ability to communicate in writing, over the telephone, and in person with office staff and insurance representatives.

2. Ability to recognize, evaluate, solve problems, and correct errors.

3. Ability to conceptualize work flow, develop plans, and implement appropriate actions.

Equipment Operated: Standard office equipment including computers, fax machines, copiers, printers, telephones, etc.

Work Environment: Position is in a well-lighted office environment. Occasional evening and weekend work.

Mental/Physical Requirements: Daily activity is 80 percent sitting and 20 percent walking or standing.

Chief Executive Officer

Job Title: Chief Executive Officer

Department: Administration

Immediate Supervisor Title: Board of Directors

Job Supervisory Responsibilities: All department managers and directors

General Summary: An exempt position responsible for leading and directing all operations and related lines of business.

Essential Job Responsibilities:
1. Responsible for developing and implementing the clinic's mission and strategic plan.
2. Develops and updates organizational design for maximum productivity and control of quality and costs.
3. Ensures the financial viability of the clinic by maintaining control systems to control finances and staffing.
4. Ensures clinic compliance with all regulatory agencies governing health care delivery and the rules of accrediting bodies. Continually monitors operations, programs, physical properties. Initiates appropriate changes.
5. Represents the clinic in its relationships with other health organizations, government agencies, and third-party payers.
6. Serves as liaison and channel of communication between the board and its committees, the medical and administrative staffs.

Education: Graduate degree in health care administration or business administration.

Experience: Seven years of executive-level experience, including five years of experience in health care administration.

Other Requirements: None

Performance Requirements: *Knowledge:*

1. Thorough understanding of the health care environment.
2. Specific knowledge of finance, marketing, human resource management, and public relations in health care.

Skills:

1. Skill in exercising a high degree of initiative, judgment, discretion, and decision-making to achieve clinic's mission.
2. Skill in establishing and maintaining effective working relationships with employees, policy-making bodies, third-party payers, patients, and the public.
3. Skill in organizing work, delegating, and achieving goals and objectives.

Abilities:

1. Ability to identify trends and motivate workforce toward changes needed to adopt and remain competitive.
2. Ability to identify opportunities for improvement and change.
3. Ability to communicate and collaborate with staff, government officials, and the public.
4. Ability to guide management in its responsibilities while maintaining commitment to effective team functioning.

Equipment Operated: Standard office equipment including computers, fax machines, copiers, printers, telephones, etc.

Work Environment: Position is in a well-lighted office environment. Occasional evening and weekend work.

Mental/Physical Requirements: Involves sitting approximately 90 percent of the day, walking or standing the remainder.

Chief Operating Officer

Job Title: Chief Operating Officer

Department: Administration

Immediate Supervisor Title: Chief Executive Officer

Job Supervisory Responsibilities: All operations managers and staff

General Summary: An exempt, executive management position responsible for planning, organizing, and directing all operations.

Essential Job Responsibilities:
1. Oversees the daily operations of the organization.
2. Assists chief executive officer in developing and implementing the strategic long- and short-range plans and its business plan.
3. Represents clinic and interacts with regulatory agencies, insurance carriers, and other professional and community groups.
4. Negotiates with managed care plans and ensures the clinic's long-term financial stability.
5. Maintains compliance with governmental regulations and industry requirements.
6. Enhances operational effectiveness, emphasizing cost containment and high-quality patient care.

Education: Master's degree in health care administration, business administration, or public administration.

Experience: Minimum five years of health care management experience of at least senior-management level.

Other Requirements: Licensure or ability to obtain licensure when background credentials warrant that such is required.

Performance Requirements: *Knowledge:*

1. Knowledge of policies and procedures to manage operations and ensure effective patient care.
2. Knowledge of the principles and practices of health care administration, fiscal management, and government regulations and reimbursements.

Skills:

1. Skill in exercising a high degree of initiative, judgment, and discretion.
2. Skill in analyzing situations accurately and taking effective action.
3. Skill in establishing and maintaining effective working relationships.
4. Skill in organizing work, delegating and achieving goals and objectives.
5. Skill in exercising judgment and discretion in developing, interpreting, and implementing departmental policies and procedures.

Abilities:

1. Ability to plan, organize, and integrate priorities and deadlines.
2. Ability to identify, analyze, and resolve operational problems.
3. Ability to evaluate and make recommendations for continuous quality improvement.
4. Ability to communicate clearly and effectively orally and in writing.

Equipment Operated: Standard office equipment including computers, fax machines, copiers, printers, telephones, etc.

Work Environment: Position is in a well-lighted office environment. Occasional evening and weekend work.

Mental/Physical Requirements: Involves sitting approximately 90 percent of the day, walking or standing the remainder.

Compliance Officer

Job Title:	Compliance Officer
Department:	Administration
Immediate Supervisor Title:	Chief Executive Officer
Job Supervisory Responsibilities:	Department staff as assigned
General Summary:	An exempt, management position responsible for ensuring the organization remains in compliance with all regulations, requirements, and reporting results of compliance and ethics of the organization.
Essential Job Responsibilities:	1. Develops, initiates, maintains, and revises policies and procedures for the operation of the compliance program.
	2. Works to promote compliance with all applicable laws, regulations, rules, and policies of governmental authorities and payers.
	3. Develops and coordinates compliance education and training.
	4. Conducts and coordinates internal compliance audits and reviews. Responds to incidents of suspected compliance violations by evaluating or recommending the initiation of investigative procedures. Takes appropriate actions as approved by the chief executive officer.
Education:	Bachelor's degree in business administration or health care administration. Master's degree preferred.
Experience:	Minimum three years of experience in health care with at least one year in health care compliance.
Other Requirements:	None

Performance Requirements: *Knowledge:*

1. Extensive knowledge of health care laws, regulations, and standards.

2. Understanding of coding and reimbursements systems, risk management, and performance improvement helpful.

Skills:

1. Written and verbal communication skills.

2. Strong analytical and problem-solving skills.

3. Strong interpersonal skills.

Abilities:

1. Ability to understand and interpret insurance laws and regulations.

Equipment Operated: Standard office equipment including computers, fax machines, copiers, printers, telephones, etc.

Work Environment: Position is in a well-lighted office environment. Occasional evening and weekend work.

Mental/Physical Requirements: Involves sitting approximately 90 percent of the day, walking or standing the remainder.

Executive Assistant

Job Title:	Executive Assistant
Department:	Administration
Immediate Supervisor Title:	Chief Executive Officer
Job Supervisory Responsibilities:	None
General Summary:	A nonexempt, office position responsible for providing secretarial assistance to the chief executive officer, providing secretarial support to the Board of Directors, and performing a variety of complex clerical functions.
Essential Job Responsibilities:	1. Performs secretarial duties for executive management staff, including typing routine and confidential correspondence, drafts, reports, contracts, and memos; scheduling appointments for the chief executive officer; maintaining files of organization; typing and correspondence.
	2. Attends monthly Board of Directors meetings. Records minutes of meetings. Maintains governance documents and files including those related to committees, quality assurance, strategic planning, bylaws, personnel, compensation, finance, etc.
	3. Maintains current policies and procedures manuals as revisions are made.
Education:	High school diploma or equivalent. Further business education preferred.
Experience:	Minimum five years of office experience, including one year in a health care organization
Other Requirements:	None

Performance Requirements: *Knowledge:*

1. Knowledge of organization policies, procedures, systems.
2. Knowledge of customer service skills, both in person and over the telephone.

Skills:

1. Skill in written and verbal communication.
2. Skill in word processing.
3. Skill in shorthand, dictation, or transcription to take meeting minutes.

Abilities:

1. Ability to edit and review documents for typographical errors, omissions, or lack of clarity.
2. Ability to manage multiple and changing projects rapidly and effectively.

Equipment Operated: Standard office equipment including computers, fax machines, copiers, printers, telephones, postal machines, etc.

Work Environment: Position is in a well-lighted office environment. Occasional evening and weekend work.

Mental/Physical Requirements: Involves sitting approximately 80 percent of the day, walking or standing for the remainder. Work may require stooping and bending to access files and supplies, mobility to complete errands, and lifting up to 20 pounds.

Facilities Manager

Job Title:	Facilities Manager
Department:	Administration
Immediate Supervisor Title:	Office Manager
Job Supervisory Responsibilities:	None
General Summary:	A nonexempt position responsible for managing the physical facilities and related services including supplies; maintenance; housekeeping; security; heating, ventilation, and air conditioning (HVAC); and grounds maintenance.

Essential Job Responsibilities:

1. Oversees continued development of office and sites (exteriors and interiors), building equipment, and grounds.

2. Monitors current inventory level of supplies and contacts appropriate vendors to secure bids and place orders. Confirms delivery, quality, and quantity of orders.

3. Coordinates and schedules maintenance and cleaning activities to ensure facilities are clean, safe, sanitary, and conducive to the delivery of quality patient care.

4. Manages, coordinates, and monitors all maintenance contracts with outside vendors.

5. Oversees performance and maintains records of cyclical maintenance projects.

6. Assists and coordinates on assigned building projects, including directing repair, construction, and renovation.

7. Oversees building security and safety. Assists with development and implementation of disaster plan. Assists with training staff in use of fire extinguishers and evacuation procedures.

Education:	High school diploma; some college preferred.
Experience:	Minimum four years of experience in building/grounds maintenance, including two years experience in a health care organization.
Other Requirements:	None

Performance Requirements: *Knowledge:*

1. Knowledge of clinic policies and procedures.
2. Knowledge of federal, state, and local building standards, codes, and requirements of regulatory agencies.
3. Knowledge of standard operating procedures for clinic operation, facilities management, and engineering.
4. Knowledge of safety practices and hazardous conditions to provide a safe work environment.

Skills:

1. Skill in exercising independent judgment.
2. Skill managing contracts with subcontractors.
3. Skill in establishing and maintaining working relationships with staff and patients.

Abilities:

1. Ability to work effectively with vendors and staff.
2. Ability to communicate clearly and effectively.

Equipment Operated: Standard office equipment including computers, fax machines, copiers, printers, telephones, etc.

Work Environment: Combination of office and grounds environment. Occasional evening or weekend work.

Mental/Physical Requirements: Prolonged standing and walking; repeated bending, squatting, stooping, climbing ladders, scaffolding. May be exposed to hazards from use of electrical, electronic, mechanical, and power equipment and toxic chemicals and gases. Occasionally must lift up to 50 pounds.

Office Manager

Job Title:	Office Manager
Department:	Administration
Immediate Supervisor Title:	Chief Executive Officer
Job Supervisory Responsibilities:	All support staff
General Summary:	An exempt management position responsible for managing the daily operations of the office.
Essential Job Responsibilities:	1. Oversees daily office operations and delegates authority to assigned supervisors. 2. Assists supervisors in developing and implementing short- and long-term work plans and objectives for clerical functions. 3. Assists supervisors in understanding/implementing clinic policies and procedures. 4. Develops guidelines for prioritizing work activities, evaluating effectiveness, and modifying activities as necessary. Ensures that office is staffed appropriately. 5. Assists in the recruiting, hiring, orientation, development, and evaluation of clerical staff. 6. Establishes and maintains an efficient and responsive patient flow system. 7. Oversees and approves office supply inventory, ensures that mail is opened and processed, and offices are opened and closed according to procedures. 8. Supports and upholds established policies, procedures, objectives, quality improvement, safety, environmental and infection control, and codes and requirements of accreditation and regulatory agencies.
Education:	Bachelor's degree, preferably with coursework in health care administration.
Experience:	Minimum three years of administrative experience, including one year of management experience in health care.
Other Requirements:	None

Performance Requirements: *Knowledge:*

    1. Knowledge of medical practices, terminology, and reimbursement policies.

    Skills:

    1. Skill in planning, organizing, delegating, and supervising.

    2. Skill in evaluating the effectiveness of existing methods and procedures.

    3. Skill in problem solving.

    4. Skill in verbal and written communication.

    Abilities:

    1. Ability to read, interpret, and apply policies and procedures.

    2. Ability to set priorities among multiple requests.

    3. Ability to interact with patients, medical and administrative staff, and the public effectively.

Equipment Operated: Standard office equipment including computers, fax machines, copiers, printers, telephones, etc.

Work Environment: Position is in a well-lighted office environment. Occasional evening and weekend work.

Mental/Physical Requirements: Involves sitting approximately 90 percent of the day, walking or standing the remainder.

Receptionist

Job Title:	Receptionist
Department:	Administration
Immediate Supervisor Title:	Office Manager
Job Supervisory Responsibilities:	None
General Summary:	A nonexempt, clerical position responsible for receiving incoming telephone calls in a prompt, courteous, and professional manner and greeting/assisting visitors in the same manner.
Essential Job Responsibilities:	1. Promptly and professionally answers telephone calls. Routes calls appropriately, offering voice mail, paging, or redirection of calls as needed.
	2. Greets visitors and assists them as appropriate. Phones or pages employees to meet visitors, directs visitors to appropriate waiting areas, and appropriately and courteously screen solicitors for relevance to organization needs.
	3. Explains financial requirements to the patients or responsible parties and collects copays as required.
	4. Other duties as assigned.
Education:	High school diploma or equivalent.
Experience:	One year of experience in customer service or reception, preferably in a health care environment.
Other Requirements:	None

Performance Requirements: *Knowledge:*

1. Knowledge of medical terminology and organization services.
2. Knowledge of individual responsibilities to accurately direct callers.

Skills:

1. Ability to use multi-line phone system, including transferring calls and paging.
2. Adequate hearing to answer phone and speak with patients.
3. Ability to speak clearly and loudly enough to be heard by callers and patients.

Abilities:

1. Elicits appropriate information to route calls to the appropriate person.
2. Prevents, calms, or defuses irate callers and patients by working with them to identify concerns and properly directs calls.

Equipment Operated: Standard office equipment including computers, fax machines, copiers, printers, telephones, etc.

Work Environment: Position is in a well-lighted office environment. Occasional evening and weekend work.

Mental/Physical Requirements: Involves sitting approximately 90 percent of the day, walking or standing the remainder.

Satellite Operations Supervisor

Job Title: Satellite Operations Supervisor

Department: Administration

Immediate Supervisor Title: Chief Executive Officer

Job Supervisory Responsibilities: Management and support staff of satellite offices

General Summary: An exempt, management position responsible for directing, supervising, and coordinating staff and activities at satellite offices to provide quality, cost-effective care.

Essential Job Responsibilities:
1. Manages daily operations at satellite offices and coordinates the work activities and schedules.
2. Ensures provisions of safe, high-quality patient care by the staff.
3. Evaluates performance and recommends merit increases, promotions, and disciplinary actions.
4. Ensures that office space, supplies, equipment, and assistance are provided and maintained appropriately for medical staff and patient care.
5. Ensures that all business functions are operative and that all processes are effectively and efficiently in place. Reviews processes and makes recommendations for improvement. Creates goals for satellite operations and ensures that these goals are in line with organization goals.
6. Operates within the context of an established budget. Makes recommendations for annual budget and maximizes opportunities to meet and exceed budget guidelines.

Education: Bachelor's degree in health or business administration. Master's degree in health care, business administration, or related field preferred.

Experience: Three to five years of office management experience including at least two years in a health care organization.

Other Requirements: None

Performance Requirements: *Knowledge:*

1. Knowledge of organization policies and procedures.
2. Knowledge of fiscal management and human resource management techniques.
3. Knowledge of office management techniques and practices.

Skills:

1. Excellent organizational and time management skills.
2. Outstanding verbal and written communication skills.
3. Setting, defining, assigning, monitoring, and evaluating outcomes of tasks and goals.

Abilities:

1. Ability to clearly communicate and apply policies and principles to solve everyday problems and deal with a variety of situations.
2. Ability to plan, exercise initiative, problem solve, make decisions.
3. Ability to read, interpret, and apply clinic policies and procedures.
4. Ability to identify problems and recommend solutions.
5. Ability to establish priorities and coordinate work activities.
6. Ability to manage financial information.

Equipment Operated: Standard office equipment including computers, fax machines, copiers, printers, telephones, etc.

Work Environment: Position is in a well-lighted office environment. Occasional evening and weekend work.

Mental/Physical Requirements: Involves sitting approximately 80 percent of the day, walking or standing the remainder.

FINANCE

- Accounting Clerk
- Accounting Manager
- Chief Financial Officer
- Claims Analyst
- Collections Agent
- Controller
- Credit Manager
- Managed Care Analyst
- Medical Billing/Coding Specialist
- Medicare Coordinator
- Payroll Administrator
- Payroll Clerk
- Reimbursement Specialist
- Senior Accountant
- Staff Accountant

Accounting Clerk

Job Title: Accounting Clerk

Department: Finance

Immediate Supervisor Title: Accounting Manager

Job Supervisory Responsibilities: None

General Summary: A nonexempt position responsible for accounting functions and transactions.

Essential Job Responsibilities:
1. Assists in preparing monthly financial and cost reports.
2. Assists in posting information to general ledger.
3. Assists in reconciling general ledger.
4. Processes all accounts payable invoices.
5. Processes accounts payable checks and voided checks.

Education: High school diploma or equivalent. Some accounting courses preferred.

Experience: Minimum two years of accounts payable experience, preferably in health care and exposure to general ledger accounting.

Other Requirements: None

Performance Requirements: *Knowledge:*

1. Knowledge of accounting systems and the generally accepted accounting principles.
2. Knowledge of basic mathematics.

Skills:

1. Accurate data entry skills.
2. Good communication skills with both internal and external customers.
3. Good organization skills and keen attention to detail.

Abilities:

1. Ability to examine documents for accuracy and completeness.
2. Ability to understand and interpret policies and regulations.

Equipment Operated: Standard office equipment including computers, fax machines, copiers, printers, telephones, etc.

Work Environment: Position is in a well-lighted office environment. Occasional evening and weekend work.

Mental/Physical Requirements: Involves sitting approximately 90 percent of the day, walking or standing the remainder.

Accounting Manager

Job Title: Accounting Manager

Department: Finance

Immediate Supervisor Title: Chief Financial Officer

Job Supervisory Responsibilities: Designated individuals in the accounting department

General Summary: An exempt position responsible for assisting in determining financial objectives; analyzing and reporting accounting variances; developing and monitoring accounting reports and control mechanisms.

Essential Job Responsibilities:
1. Directs and coordinates activities of accounting staff including payroll, accounts payable, general ledger, tax payments, fixes assets, and purchasing activities.
2. Develops, implements, and maintains accounting policies and procedures regarding patient accounts and reimbursements by patient, insurance, and other third-party reimbursers.
3. Closes the monthly financial records according to generally accepted accounting principles, which include preparing journal entries, reconciling accounting, and functioning as the primary accountant.
4. Oversees operating budgets and ensures expenditures do not exceed budgetary limits.
5. Prepares for and assists in the annual independent audit of the organization by the accounting firm.

Education: Bachelor's degree in accounting or finance.

Experience: Minimum three years of experience in accounting management, including two years in a health care organization.

Other Requirements: CPA preferred.

Performance Requirements: *Knowledge:*

1. Knowledge of advanced financial accounting, analysis, and reporting to design, modify, and manage an accounting system.

2. Knowledge of automated accounting systems and governmental regulations.

3. Knowledge of reimbursement procedures to compile and allocate cost information to specific accounts.

Skills:

1. Skill in budgeting, preparing financial reports, and computer applications.

2. Skill in exercising initiative, judgment, discretion, and decision-making to achieve organizational objectives.

3. Skill in identifying and resolving accounting problems.

Abilities:

1. Ability to delegate responsibility and authority to staff.

2. Ability to work creatively with management and department staff to achieve objectives.

3. Ability to communicate effectively with all levels of management regarding financial policies.

Equipment Operated: Standard office equipment including computers, fax machines, copiers, printers, telephones, etc.

Work Environment: Position is in a well-lighted office environment. Occasional evening and weekend work.

Mental/Physical Requirements: Involves sitting approximately 90 percent of the day, walking or standing the remainder.

Chief Financial Officer

Job Title:	Chief Financial Officer
Department:	Finance
Immediate Supervisor Title:	Chief Executive Officer
Job Supervisory Responsibilities:	Controller, accounting manager, senior accountant, and business office manager; indirect supervision of all members of the finance department
General Summary:	An exempt position responsible for directing the organization's financial planning and accounting practices as well as its relationship with lending institutions, pay sources, and the financial community.

Essential Job Responsibilities:

1. Interacts with clinic management staff in developing the strategic plan and its financial planning component.
2. Oversees and directs budgeting, audit, tax, accounting, purchasing, long-range forecasting, and insurance activities for the organization.
3. Evaluates the organization's financial position and issues periodic reports on the organization's financial stability, liquidity, and growth.
4. Develops and implements financial policies and procedures and ensures compliance.
5. Assures implementation of internal controls and generally accepted accounting procedures accounting.
6. Supervises the analysis of costs and makes rate recommendations to ensure appropriate income/cash flow.
7. Oversees and directs the preparation and issuance of the organization's annual tax and other reports. Prepares or reviews financial statements for Board of Directors.

Education:	Master's degree in business administration, accounting, or finance.
Experience:	Eight to 10 years of experience in financial/accounting management. Experience in health care financial management strongly preferred.
Other Requirements:	CPA required.

Performance Requirements:	*Knowledge:*

Knowledge:

1. Knowledge of the principles of financial management sufficient to direct professional staff and coordinate all aspects involved with fiscal requirements.

2. Knowledge of clinic financial and budgetary practices to develop annual budget, analyze financial data and patterns, and prepare financial statements.

3. Knowledge of clinic's strategic business objectives and employee performance objectives.

4. Knowledge of governmental and health care fiscal regulations and reporting requirements.

Skills:

1. Skill in exercising a high degree of initiative, judgment, discretion, and decision-making to achieve objectives.

2. Skill in evaluating operations as they relate to policies, goals and objectives, costs, and rate levels.

3. Skill in establishing and maintaining effective working relationships with patients, medical staff, and the public.

4. Skill in identifying and resolving accounting and financial problems.

Abilities:

1. Ability to create an atmosphere that encourages motivation, innovation, and high performance.

2. Ability to delegate responsibility and authority to staff.

3. Ability to communicate effectively and clearly.

Equipment Operated: Standard office equipment including computers, fax machines, copiers, printers, telephones, etc.

Work Environment: Position is in a well-lighted office environment. Occasional evening and weekend work.

Mental/Physical Requirements: Involves sitting approximately 90 percent of the day, walking or standing the remainder.

Claims Analyst

Job Title:	Claims Analyst
Department:	Finance
Immediate Supervisor Title:	Chief Financial Officer or Controller
Job Supervisory Responsibilities:	None
General Summary:	A nonexempt position responsible for the proper and timely processing of claims and payments to providers.

Essential Job Responsibilities:

1. Oversees claim processing and payments to third-party providers. Answers associated correspondence.
2. Monitors charges and verifies correct payment of claims and capitation deductions.
3. Sends denial letters on claims and follows up on requests for information.
4. Audits and reviews claim payments reports for accuracy and compliance.
5. Researches and resolves claim and capitation problems.
6. Prepares claim reports for administration and finance on utilization and claim payment turnaround time. Identifies exceptional claims for review.
7. Initiates payment recovery for stop loss reinsurance, worker's compensation, and overpaid claims.

Education:	Bachelor's degree in health or business administration.
Experience:	Minimum two years of experience in claims processing in a health care setting.
Other Requirements:	None

Performance Requirements: *Knowledge:*

1. Knowledge of clinic policies and procedures.
2. Knowledge of health care insurance claim practices and compliance.
3. Knowledge of computer systems, programs, and applications.
4. Knowledge of medical terminology.

Skills:

1. Skill in gathering and reporting claim information.
2. Skill in trouble-shooting claim insurance problems.
3. Skill in written and verbal communication and customer relations.

Abilities:

1. Ability to work effectively with physicians, other medical staff, and external agencies.
2. Ability to identify and analyze claim problems.

Equipment Operated: Standard office equipment including computers, fax machines, copiers, printers, telephones, etc.

Work Environment: Position is in a well-lighted office environment. Occasional evening and weekend work.

Mental/Physical Requirements: Involves sitting approximately 90 percent of the day, walking or standing the remainder.

Collections Agent

Job Title:	Collections Agent
Department:	Finance
Immediate Supervisor Title:	Credit Manager
Job Supervisory Responsibilities:	None
General Summary:	A nonexempt position responsible for collection of delinquent patient accounts.

Essential Job Responsibilities:

1. Identifies delinquent accounts, aging period, and payment sources. Processes delinquent unpaid accounts by contacting patients and third-party reimbursers.

2. Reviews accounts, credit reports, and other information sources such as credit bureaus via computer.

3. Performs various collection actions including contacting patients by phone and resubmitting claims to third-party reimbursers.

4. Evaluates patient financial status and establishes budget payment plans. Follows and reports status of delinquent accounts.

5. Reviews accounts for possible assignment; makes recommendations to credit manager and prepares information for collection agency.

6. Assigns uncollectible accounts to collection agency or attorney via clinic credit and collection policy. Contacts lawyers involved in third-party litigation.

Education:	High school diploma or equivalent. Some college preferred.
Experience:	Minimum two years of medical collections experience.
Other Requirements:	None

Performance Requirements: *Knowledge:*

1. Knowledge of medical billing/collection practices.

2. Knowledge of basic medical coding and third-party operating procedures and practices.

3. Knowledge of legal and regulatory government provisions.

Skills:

1. Skill in establishing and maintaining effective internal and external working relationships.

Abilities:

1. Ability to enter accurately data and examine insurance documents.

2. Ability to deal courteously with patients, staff, and others.

3. Ability to communicate effectively and clearly.

Equipment Operated: Standard office equipment including computers, fax machines, copiers, printers, telephones, etc.

Work Environment: Position is in a well-lighted office environment. Occasional evening and weekend work.

Mental/Physical Requirements: Involves sitting approximately 90 percent of the day, walking or standing the remainder.

Controller

Job Title:	Controller
Department:	Finance
Immediate Supervisor Title:	Chief Financial Officer
Job Supervisory Responsibilities:	Finance department staff
General Summary:	An exempt position responsible for organizing and maintaining financial accounting systems, including accounts payable, general ledger, accounts receivable, employee payroll, cash disbursements, financial statements, and tax information.

Essential Job Responsibilities:

1. Develops and plans department objectives with chief financial officer and staff including short- and long-range accounting programs in budgeting, profit analysis, accounting systems, Medicare cost reporting, and internal auditing.

2. Directs financial accounting functions to ensure timely and accurate reporting of financial information. Develops and implements policies and procedures to ensure compliance with regulatory agencies.

3. Works with finance director to develop and approve financial statements, including balance sheets, profit/loss statements, and analysis of variances in accounts, ratios, income/expense, as well as investment analysis, e.g., effects of fee changes on costs and profits, return on investment.

4. Reviews all third-party contracts and monitors contract revenues. Interacts with auditors, lenders, and other third-party agencies regarding accounting functions.

5. Develops and monitors the internal audit program to ensure internal financial controls. Oversees the annual financial audit and any other special audits.

6. Directs the preparation of statistical information and reports for management, government, and other agencies.

Education:	Bachelor's degree in finance or accounting. Master's degree in finance preferred.
Experience:	Minimum three years of financial management experience including two years in a health care organization.
Other Requirements:	CPA preferred.

Performance Requirements: *Knowledge:*

1. Knowledge of finance and accounting functions, including budgeting, credit, investments, and internal controls.
2. Knowledge of computer systems, spreadsheet and financial systems programs and applications.
3. Knowledge of management practices to lead assigned staff.
4. Knowledge of strategic business objectives and employee performance objectives.

Skills:

1. Skill in analyzing financial data and preparing appropriate related reports.
2. Skill in relating organizational objectives to financial policies on costs, fees, credit, etc.
3. Skill in exercising initiative, judgment, discretion, and decision-making to achieve organizational objectives.
4. Skill in establishing and maintaining effective working relationships with patients, medical staff, auditors, and the public.
5. Skill in identifying and resolving accounting and financial problems.

Abilities:

1. Ability to delegate responsibility and authority to staff and work under multiple priorities.
2. Ability to work creatively with management and department staff to achieve objectives.
3. Ability to communicate effectively and clearly.

Equipment Operated: Standard office equipment including computers, fax machines, copiers, printers, telephones, etc.

Work Environment: Position is in a well-lighted office environment. Occasional evening and weekend work.

Mental/Physical Requirements: Involves sitting approximately 90 percent of the day, walking or standing the remainder.

Credit Manager

Job Title: Credit Manager

Department: Finance

Immediate Supervisor Title: Chief Financial Officer or Controller

Job Supervisory Responsibilities: Medical billing/coding specialist

General Summary: An exempt position responsible for ensuring currency of accounts receivable including monitoring for delinquent payments.

Essential Job Responsibilities:
1. Gathers data on daily, monthly, and yearly basis to determine credit status of clinic patient accounts.
2. Monitors private-pay patient accounts for delinquent payments and determines course of action.
3. Follows clinic collection policy guidelines and refers to collection agency upon physician approval.
4. Uses collection management reports to keep accounts receivable current.
5. Runs routine insurance claim forms and statements to check on credit status.
6. Assists with filing claims in cases of bankruptcy or to estates of deceased patients for unpaid accounts.

Education: Bachelor's degree in business administration or related field.

Experience: Minimum three years of collection and management experience in a health care organization.

Other Requirements: None

Performance Requirements:
Knowledge:

1. Knowledge of collection methods, policies, and procedures.
2. Knowledge of calculations to compute fees and interest.

Skills:

1. Skill in using computer programs, spreadsheets, and applications for credit entry, retrieval, and modification.
2. Skill in supervising staff and serving as resource to management.

Abilities:

1. Ability to understand and interpret credit policies and regulations.
2. Ability to respond to patients on credit matters in courteous fashion.
3. Ability to examine medical documents for accuracy and completeness.
4. Ability to communicate effectively and clearly.

Equipment Operated: Standard office equipment including computers, fax machines, copiers, printers, telephones, etc.

Work Environment: Position is in a well-lighted office environment. Occasional evening and weekend work.

Mental/Physical Requirements: Involves sitting approximately 90 percent of the day, walking or standing the remainder.

Managed Care Analyst

Job Title: Managed Care Analyst

Department: Finance

Immediate Supervisor Title: Chief Financial Officer or Controller

Job Supervisory Responsibilities: None

General Summary: A nonexempt position responsible for analyzing utilization data from health plans' claims.

Essential Job Responsibilities:
1. Analyzes, prepares, and reports on medical service contracts and utilization data.
2. Updates patient database. Prepares and reports on patient statistics.
3. Prepares capitation payments and recalculates capitation rates for subcontracts and specialists.
4. Prepares and explains managed care comparison reports.
5. Submits claims data, inputs into database, and files documentation.
6. Calculates health plan discounts.

Education: Bachelor's degree in health or business administration preferred.

Experience: Minimum one year of health care experience in claims and customer service.

Other Requirements: None

Performance Requirements: *Knowledge:*

1. Knowledge of clinic policies and procedures.

2. Knowledge of managed care contracts and utilization.

3. Knowledge of computer systems, programs, and spreadsheet applications.

4. Knowledge of medical terminology.

Skills:

1. Skill in gathering and reporting claim information.

2. Skill in solving utilization problems.

3. Skill in written and verbal communication and customer relations.

Abilities:

1. Ability to work effectively with medical staff and external agencies.

2. Ability to identify, analyze, and solve claim problems.

Equipment Operated: Standard office equipment including computers, fax machines, copiers, printers, telephones, etc.

Work Environment: Position is in a well-lighted office environment. Occasional evening and weekend work.

Mental/Physical Requirements: Involves sitting approximately 90 percent of the day, walking or standing the remainder.

Medical Billing/Coding Specialist

Job Title:	Medical Billing/Coding Specialist
Department:	Finance
Immediate Supervisor Title:	Accounting Manager
Job Supervisory Responsibilities:	None
General Summary:	A nonexempt position responsible for coordinating, verifying, distributing, and managing all billable services.
Essential Job Responsibilities:	1. Coordinates with clinical staff to get charge information for all patients.
	2. Codes information about procedures performed and diagnosis on charge.
	3. Verifies and completes charge information in database and produces billing.
	4. Processes and distributes copies of billings according to clinic policies.
	5. Maintains required billing records, reports, files, etc.
Education:	High school diploma or equivalent; some college preferred.
Experience:	Minimum one year of billing experience in a health care organization.
Other Requirements:	None

Performance Requirements:	*Knowledge:*
	1. Knowledge of billing practices and clinic policies and procedures.
	2. Knowledge of coding and clinic operating policies.

Skills:

1. Proficient skills in computer programs.
2. Skill in using a calculator.

Abilities:

1. Ability to understand and interpret policies and regulations.
2. Ability to read and interpret medical charts.
3. Ability to examine documents for accuracy and completeness.
4. Ability to communicate effectively and work with others.

Equipment Operated:	Standard office equipment including computers, fax machines, copiers, printers, telephones, calculators, etc.
Work Environment:	Position is in a well-lighted office environment. Occasional evening and weekend work.
Mental/Physical Requirements:	Requires sitting and standing associated with a normal office environment. Manual dexterity using calculator.

Medicare Coordinator

Job Title: Medicare Coordinator

Department: Finance

Immediate Supervisor Title: Chief Financial Officer or Controller

Job Supervisory Responsibilities: None

General Summary: A nonexempt position responsible for assisting with and monitoring the delivery of care and tracking for the Medicare populations.

Essential Job Responsibilities:
1. Assists physicians and other providers in assessing the optimal level, type, and mix of medical care for Medicare patients.
2. Oversees Medicare Quality Improvement initiatives, identifies quality of care deficits, and assists with developing interventions to ensure treatment.
3. Coordinates geriatric disease management program; focuses on approaches to chronic illness while emphasizing efficiency and cost effectiveness.
4. Participates in disease management programs and coordinated health care plan chart reviews of Medicare risk population.

Education: Bachelor's degree in nursing.

Experience: Minimum three years of clinic and case management experience.
Geriatric experience preferred.

Other Requirements: Licensed registered nurse.

Performance Requirements: *Knowledge:*

1. Knowledge of clinic policies and procedures.
2. Knowledge of case management practices and compliance.
3. Knowledge of Medicare government and insurance requirements.

Skills:

1. Skill in gathering and analyzing Medicare information.
2. Skill in troubleshooting Medicare problems and claims.
3. Skill in written and verbal communication.

Abilities:

1. Ability to work effectively with patients, physicians, and health plan representatives.
2. Ability to identify and analyze quality care concerns.

Equipment Operated: Standard office equipment including computers, fax machines, copiers, printers, telephones, etc.

Work Environment: Position is in a well-lighted office environment. Occasional evening and weekend work.

Mental/Physical Requirements: Involves sitting approximately 90 percent of the day, walking or standing the remainder. Some bending, stooping, and lifting up to 25 pounds.

Payroll Administrator

Job Title:	Payroll Administrator
Department:	Finance
Immediate Supervisor Title:	Controller
Job Supervisory Responsibilities:	Payroll Clerk
General Summary:	An exempt position responsible for overseeing the payroll function for the organization.

Essential Job Responsibilities:

1. Establishes systems and procedures that ensure the appropriate and timely payment of employees.
2. Manages the preparation, distribution, and reporting processes for payroll.
3. Oversees the calculation of wages, overtime, and deductions to ensure compliance with federal, state, and local laws and regulations.
4. Generates reports from databases to disseminate information to internal departments and external entities.
5. Performs reconciliations of payroll information and accounting information for budgetary purposes.

Education:	College degree preferred with accounting and finance courses.
Experience:	Minimum five years of experience as a payroll administrator.
Other Requirements:	None

Performance Requirements: *Knowledge:*

1. Knowledge of complex payroll practices and wage/hour laws, including tax filing and other financial responsibilities.

2. Knowledge of state-of-the-art payroll programs and payroll systems.

3. Understanding of the principles of accounting as they relate to payroll functions.

Skills:

1. Skill in interpreting and analyzing payroll data.

2. Effective communication skills, both verbal and written.

3. Effective management skills.

Abilities:

1. Ability to accurately perform mathematical functions and statistical analysis.

2. Ability to prepare and analyze comprehensive reports.

3. Ability to maintain confidentiality of financial matters.

4. Ability to work effectively with others.

5. Ability to ensure compliance with deadlines.

Equipment Operated: Standard office equipment including computers, fax machines, copiers, printers, telephones, etc.

Work Environment: Position is in a well-lighted office environment. Occasional evening and weekend work.

Mental/Physical Requirements: Requires sitting and standing associated with a normal office environment.

Payroll Clerk

Job Title: Payroll Clerk

Department: Finance

Immediate Supervisor Title: Payroll Administrator

Job Supervisory Responsibilities: None

General Summary: A nonexempt position responsible for preparation of payroll.

Essential Job Responsibilities:
1. Processes employee time sheets and checks for accuracy. Clarifies inconsistencies with supervisors.
2. Verifies sick leave, vacation hours, and overtime by comparing authorization forms to time reports.
3. Processes COBRA, jury duty, short- and long-term disability payments.
4. Adds and deletes employees from payroll and accounting systems.
5. Processes employment verifications forms, wage assignments, levies, and child support.
6. Distributes payroll checks to the appropriate department.

Education: High school diploma; some college preferred.

Experience: Minimum two years of payroll experience.

Other Requirements: None

Performance Requirements:	*Knowledge:*
	1. Understanding of payroll practices as well as federal and state wage/hour laws.
	2. Understanding of various payroll systems.
	Skills:
	1. Must be able to multi-task and have attention to detail.
	2. Perform accurate data entry both alpha and numeric.
	Abilities:
	1. Ability to work efficiently and accurately within specific deadlines.
	2. Ability to work with and learn new systems that are implemented.
	3. Ability to prepare comprehensive reports.
	4. Ability to effectively communicate and work with other people.
Equipment Operated:	Standard office equipment including computers, fax machines, copiers, printers, telephones, etc.
Work Environment:	Position is in a well-lighted office environment. Occasional evening and weekend work.
Mental/Physical Requirements:	Involves sitting approximately 90 percent of the day, walking or standing the remainder.

Reimbursement Specialist

Job Title:	Reimbursement Specialist
Department:	Finance
Immediate Supervisor Title:	Chief Financial Officer or Controller
Job Supervisory Responsibilities:	None
General Summary:	A nonexempt position responsible for performing billings and collections for alpha, discipline, and/or payer.
Essential Job Responsibilities:	1. Reviews all claims within designated alpha and discipline before claim release.
	2. Attaches required documentation to claims for payments.
	3. Assists customers with billing questions.
	4. Researches and corrects all denials received for designated alpha and discipline.
	5. Documents all correspondence with patients, insurance carriers, and vendors.
	6. Other responsibilities as assigned.
Education:	High school diploma or equivalent. Some college preferred.
Experience:	Minimum one year of medical billing experience.
Other Requirements:	None

Performance Requirements: *Knowledge:*

1. Knowledge of medical terminology.
2. Knowledge of clinic policies and procedures.
3. Knowledge of computer systems, programs, and spreadsheet applications.

Skills:

1. Skill in oral and written communication.
2. Skill in time management and organization.

Abilities:

1. Ability to maintain confidentiality of all business/work information.
2. Ability to effectively work with others.

Equipment Operated: Standard office equipment including computers, fax machines, copiers, printers, telephones, etc.

Work Environment: Position is in a well-lighted office environment. Occasional evening and weekend work.

Mental/Physical Requirements: Involves sitting approximately 90 percent of the day, walking or standing the remainder.

Senior Accountant

Job Title:	Senior Accountant
Department:	Finance
Immediate Supervisor Title:	Accounting Manager
Job Supervisory Responsibilities:	Assigned accounting staff
General Summary:	An exempt position responsible for managing, maintaining, and analyzing accounting management information including general ledger activity through financial statements.

Essential Job Responsibilities:

1. Prepares accurate monthly financial statements.
2. Analyzes, reviews, and adjusts income and expense information as to adequacy, form, and source.
3. Maintains general ledger, including preparing financial schedules and writing journal entries for such items as interest income, prepaid insurance, FICA payments, etc.
4. Maintains cash schedules, inspects account status, transfers cash as necessary to cover disbursements.
5. Conducts reconciliations of balance sheet asset and liability accounts to ensure correctness. Identifies and resolves discrepancies.
6. Maintains amortization schedules for lease agreements, mortgages, bank notes, and bond premiums.

Education:	Bachelor's degree in accounting.
Experience:	Minimum three years of experience in professional accounting and management experience including one year in health care.
Other Requirements:	None

Performance Requirements:	*Knowledge:*
	1. Knowledge of accounting practices to understand and interpret various accounting systems.
	2. Knowledge of budgeting and cost accounting principles.
	Skills:
	1. Skill in defining problems, collecting data, interpreting financial material.
	2. Skill in preparing statistical and narrative accounting and auditing reports.
	Abilities:
	1. Ability to evaluate accounting systems.
	2. Ability to use cost accounting reports to recommend alternatives for controlling operations.
	3. Ability to perform mathematical computations and compute ratios and percentages.
	4. Ability to communicate clearly.
Equipment Operated:	Standard office equipment including computers, fax machines, copiers, printers, telephones, etc.
Work Environment:	Position is in a well-lighted office environment. Occasional evening and weekend work.
Mental/Physical Requirements:	Involves sitting approximately 90 percent of the day, walking or standing the remainder.

Staff Accountant

Job Title: Staff Accountant

Department: Finance

Immediate Supervisor Title: Accounting Manager

Job Supervisory Responsibilities: None

General Summary: A nonexempt position responsible for assisting accounting manager with accounting functions including reporting of financial operations.

Essential Job Responsibilities:
1. Prepares monthly general and standard journal entries, financial statements and comparative reports, account reconciliations, cost reports.
2. Assists independent auditors with interim and year-end audits and verifies accuracy of reports.
3. Prepares federal, state, and other governmental reports such as annual tax returns and Employee Retirement Income Security Act of 1974 (ERISA) reports.
4. Maintains and reviews cost center and appropriation accounts, including trial balances, to verify accuracy with coding, classifying, and posting.
5. Prepares reports of budget expenditures, revenues, and account or fund balances.
6. Supervises payroll activities and resolves payroll problems.

Education: Bachelor's degree in business administration, preferably in accounting.

Experience: Minimum three years of accounting experience including one year of accounting experience in health care.

Other Requirements: None

Performance Requirements:	*Knowledge:*
	1. Knowledge of the generally accepted accounting principles.
	2. Knowledge of budgeting and cost accounting principles.

Skills:

1. Excellent analytical and math skills.
2. Good communication skills.
3. Skill in dealing with multiple projects and interruptions.
4. Strong organizational skills; attention to detail.

Abilities:

1. Ability to analyze financial reports.
2. Ability to prepare accounting reports.
3. Ability to work independently and meet deadlines as assigned.
4. Ability to maintain effective working relationships.

Equipment Operated:	Standard office equipment including computers, fax machines, copiers, printers, telephones, etc.
Work Environment:	Position is in a well-lighted office environment. Occasional evening and weekend work.
Mental/Physical Requirements:	Involves sitting approximately 90 percent of the day, walking or standing the remainder.

HUMAN RESOURCES

- Benefits Specialist
- Compensation Specialist
- Human Resources Assistant
- Human Resources Director
- Human Resources Manager
- Recruiting Specialist
- Training Specialist

Benefits Specialist

Job Title:	Benefits Specialist
Department:	Human Resources
Immediate Supervisor Title:	Human Resources Manager or Human Resources Director
Job Supervisory Responsibilities:	None
General Summary:	A nonexempt position responsible for coordinating and administrating all employee benefits programs.

Essential Job Responsibilities:

1. Coordinates and administers health, dental, and life insurance plans; disability; flexible spending accounts; retirement savings plan; profit sharing programs; tuition reimbursement; COBRA; and personal leaves of absence.
2. Review for accuracy and maintains the human resources database.
3. Creates reports regarding benefits.
4. Develops and conducts new employee orientation session for new hires to explain benefit packages available.
5. Ensures compliance with medical practice policies and procedures and federal, state, and local laws and regulations.
6. Other duties as assigned.

Education:	Bachelor's degree, preferably in business or related area.
Experience:	Minimum three years of experience in human resources in a health care setting, preferably with experience in benefits.
Other Requirements:	None

Performance Requirements: *Knowledge:*

1. Knowledge of current benefits and administration requirements.

2. Knowledge of federal, state, and local regulations related to benefits.

3. Knowledge of human resources policies and procedures.

Skills:

1. Skill in using database software for benefits.

2. Skill in understanding employment law by accurate recording and reporting in compliance with regulations.

3. Skill in working with computers and computer applications.

Abilities:

1. Ability to work effectively with all levels of personnel including physicians, managers, and other staff.

2. Ability to be highly efficient, organized, and accurate in work.

Equipment Operated: Standard office equipment including computers, fax machines, copiers, printers, telephones, etc.

Work Environment: Position is in a well-lighted office environment. Occasional evening and weekend work.

Mental/Physical Requirements: Involves sitting approximately 90 percent of the day, walking or standing the remainder.

Compensation Specialist

Job Title: Compensation Specialist

Department: Human Resources

Immediate Supervisor Title: Human Resources Director or Human Resources Manager

Job Supervisory Responsibilities: None

General Summary: A nonexempt position responsible for coordinating the compensation program.

Essential Job Responsibilities:
1. Manages and maintains the payroll system.
2. Facilitates promotion/transfer functions related to salaries.
3. Analyzes current health care compensation trends and recommends changes as needed.
4. Maintains compliance with federal, state, and local employment laws and regulations.
5. Maintains all staff and personnel files.

Education: Bachelor's degree, preferably in business.

Experience: Minimum two years of experience in human resources, preferably in a health care setting. Compensation background desirable.

Other Requirements: None

Performance Requirements: *Knowledge:*

1. Knowledge of current compensation and administration requirements.
2. Knowledge of federal, state, and local regulations related to compensation and employment laws.
3. Knowledge of payroll systems.

Skills:

1. Skill in using compensation and payroll systems.
2. Skill in understanding employment law by accurate recording and reports in compliance with regulations.

Abilities:

1. Ability to work effectively with all levels of personnel including physicians, managers, and other staff.
2. Ability to be highly efficient, organized, and accurate in work.

Equipment Operated: Standard office equipment including computers, fax machines, copiers, printers, telephones, etc.

Work Environment: Position is in a well-lighted office environment. Occasional evening and weekend work.

Mental/Physical Requirements: Involves sitting approximately 90 percent of the day, walking or standing the remainder.

Human Resources Assistant

Job Title:	Human Resources Assistant
Department:	Human Resources
Immediate Supervisor Title:	Human Resources Director and/or Human Resources Manager
Job Supervisory Responsibilities:	None
General Summary:	A non-exempt clerical position responsible for functions related to payroll, personnel information, and employee documentation.
Essential Job Responsibilities:	1. Ensures new employees receive appropriate items including security card, time card, insurance/benefit information, orientation materials. Creates photo ID. Adds data to employee census.
	2. Ensures terminated employee data are removed from appropriate employee databases, including insurance/benefits, time/leave data, employee census, and file is moved to inactive status.
	3. Maintains employee address and phone extension lists and emergency contact information.
	4. Coordinates special events including employee birthdays, holiday get-togethers, and other special events.
	5. Participates in annual open enrollment benefit period and processes benefit documents.
	6. Other duties as assigned.
Education:	High school diploma. Some college preferred.
Experience:	Minimum two years of experience in administrative assistant position, preferably in health care.
Other Requirements:	None

Performance Requirements: *Knowledge:*

1. Knowledge of payroll and employment documentation.

2. Knowledge of how to use computers and human resources software applications.

3. Knowledge of employee benefits.

Skills:

1. Skill in using human resources computer capabilities including database management software.

2. Skill in clear presentation of benefits information.

Abilities:

1. Ability to establish/maintain effective relationships with staff at all levels.

2. Ability to handle sensitive and confidential employee information in a professional manner.

3. Ability to plan and coordinate multiple administrative projects.

Equipment Operated: Standard office equipment including computers, fax machines, copiers, printers, telephones, etc.

Work Environment: Position is in a well-lighted office environment. Occasional evening and weekend work.

Mental/Physical Requirements: Involves sitting approximately 90 percent of the day, walking or standing the remainder.

Human Resources Director

Job Title:	Human Resources Director
Department:	Human Resources
Immediate Supervisor Title:	Chief Executive Officer or Administrator
Job Supervisory Responsibilities:	Human Resources Manager, Human Resources Assistant, Compensation Specialist, Recruiting Specialist, Benefits Specialist, Training Specialist
General Summary:	An exempt, management position responsible for directing and coordinating the policies and practices of human resources including staffing, compensation, benefits administration, and Equal Employment Opportunity Commission (EEOC).

Essential Job Responsibilities:

1. Ensures the development of departmental plans, goals, mission, policies/ procedures, budget. Ensures selection, training, monitoring, and evaluation of departmental staff.

2. Develops/implements human resources plan for clinic including recruitment, selection, promotion/transfer, orientation, compensation administration, and labor relations in collaboration with management team. Educates/advises administrative and clinical managers on personnel issues including termination, labor disputes, morale.

3. Oversees the conduct of compensation surveys and recommends changes to ensure clinic remains competitive with market rates for wages/salaries and benefits.

4. Maintains/monitors records of worker's compensation, equal employment opportunity (EEO), Americans with Disabilities Act (ADA), Family Medical Leave Act (FMLA), unemployment, and other employee claims. Reviews exit interview data. Recommends changes to policy and training to ensure compliance with laws and regulations.

5. Practices open-door policy to encourage employees to discuss grievances. Facilitates peer-to-peer and employee–manager discussion/mediations.

6. Recommends and facilitates employee recognition efforts and events. Ensures employee assistance is available for emergency relief.

Education:	Bachelor's degree in business administration or human resources. MBA is preferred.
Experience:	Minimum seven years of experience in personnel management with progressively increasing level of responsibility. Minimum two years in the health care industry.
Other Requirements:	None

Performance Requirements:	*Knowledge:*

Knowledge:

1. Knowledge of federal and state employment/labor laws, clinic policies.
2. Knowledge of how to conduct wage/salary and employee satisfaction surveys; to mediate personnel grievances/disputes; to analyze human resources data for critical indicators.
3. Knowledge of compensation/benefits administration.

Skills:

1. Skill in staying abreast of the latest employment, labor, compensation, government regulations related to personnel.
2. Skill in gathering/analyzing objective and subjective data on personnel matters and facilitation resolution.
3. Skill in advising/educating managers on human resources best practices including employee training, motivation, development, discipline/ termination.

Abilities:

1. Ability to role model effectively with many types of people at all levels including as an employee advocate, a manager counsel, and a physician resource.
2. Ability to direct the best use of the human resources management information system in reporting statistics.
3. Ability to communicate effectively in written and verbal form.

Equipment Operated: Standard office equipment including computers, fax machines, copiers, printers, telephones, etc.

Work Environment: Position is in a well-lighted office environment. Occasional evening and weekend work.

Mental/Physical Requirements: Involves sitting approximately 90 percent of the day, walking or standing the remainder.

Human Resources Manager

Job Title:	Human Resources Manager
Department:	Human Resources
Immediate Supervisor Title:	Human Resources Director
Job Supervisory Responsibilities:	Human Resources Assistant
General Summary:	An exempt, professional position responsible for overseeing workers' compensation, employee safety, retirement programs, certain employee benefit programs, and general human resources matters.

Essential Job Responsibilities:

1. Serves as a resource to managers and staff on human resource issues.
2. Oversees worker's compensation program. Reviews and processes workers' compensation claims. Serves as a liaison between insurance carrier and medical practice.
3. Performs safety inspections to ensure a safe working environment. Addresses potential risks and implements plan to correct risk.
4. Oversees administration of medical practice retirement savings plans including 401(k) and profit-sharing programs.
5. Other duties as assigned.

Education:	Bachelor's degree in human resources or related field.
Experience:	Minimum three years of experience in human resources, preferably in the health care industry.
Other Requirements:	None

Performance Requirements:	*Knowledge:*
	1. Knowledge of worker's compensation regulations and statutes.
	2. Knowledge of human resources management practices and principles.
	3. Knowledge of federal, state, and local employment laws and regulations.

Skills:
1. Skill in computer and spreadsheet applications.
2. Skill in effective oral and written communication.

Abilities:
1. Ability to analyze and interpret data from reports.
2. Ability to work under pressure to ensure compliance.
3. Ability to develop and maintain effective working relationships.

Equipment Operated: Standard office equipment including computers, fax machines, copiers, printers, telephones, etc.

Work Environment: Position is in a well-lighted office environment. Occasional evening and weekend work.

Mental/Physical Requirements: Involves sitting approximately 90 percent of the day, walking or standing the remainder.

Recruiting Specialist

Job Title:	Recruiting Specialist
Department:	Human Resources
Immediate Supervisor Title:	Human Resources Director or Human Resources Manager
Job Supervisory Responsibilities:	None
General Summary:	A nonexempt position responsible for developing and implementing the full cycle of recruitment from the initial point of contact with qualified candidates through hiring.

Essential Job Responsibilities:

1. Works with department directors and managers to identify professional staff needs and to develop a strategic recruitment plan.
2. Actively advertises job openings using multiple media types including internal job posting boards, the Internet, job fairs, university career centers, job placement firms, national and local newspapers, and networking.
3. Responsible for reviewing applicants and screening potential candidates including initial screening interviews.
4. Reviews and checks all candidate references.
5. Other duties as assigned.

Education:	Bachelor's degree in business or related field.
Experience:	Minimum two years of experience in recruitment, preferably in a health care cnvironment.
Other Requirements:	None

Performance Requirements: *Knowledge:*

1. Knowledge of employment laws.
2. Knowledge of various recruitment methods.
3. Knowledge of customer service techniques.

Skills:

1. Skill in problem solving.
2. Skill in developing and implementing recruitment materials.
3. Excellent organizational skills.

Abilities:

1. Ability to project positive and professional image.
2. Ability to coordinate and prioritize multiple tasks, projects, and schedules.
3. Ability to establish and develop effective working relationships.

Equipment Operated: Standard office equipment including computers, fax machines, copiers, printers, telephones, etc.

Work Environment: Position is in a well-lighted office environment. Occasional evening and weekend work.

Mental/Physical Requirements: Involves sitting approximately 90 percent of the day, walking or standing the remainder.

Training Specialist

Job Title:	Training Specialist
Department:	Human Resources
Immediate Supervisor Title:	Human Resources Director or Human Resources Manager
Job Supervisory Responsibilities:	None
General Summary:	A nonexempt position responsible for the assessment of professional educational needs and for the development, implementation, and evaluation of all education and training programs.
Essential Job Responsibilities:	1. Regularly assesses the training needs of staff using interviews, surveys, observation, audits, and quality improvement data and facilitates the development of departmental training goals.
	2. Consults with department directors and managers on problems that can be solved through training.
	3. Facilitates training and orientation of new hires.
	4. Serves as an instructor for a variety of training programs when qualified. Coordinates external professional training if needed.
	5. Gathers and makes available appropriate training resources (e.g., books, DVDs, online resources) for professional development and personal use.
	6. Gathers and analyzes progress and results from training programs and prepares reports on findings.
Education:	Master's degree in education, health education, or human resource development.
Experience:	Minimum five years of experience in health education management, with three years of experience in the health care industry.
Other Requirements:	None

Performance Requirements: *Knowledge:*

1. Knowledge of instructional adult learning techniques and equipment, human resources development and quality management concepts.

2. Knowledge of current trends and issues in professional training and development.

3. Knowledge of how to identify education and training needs in health care setting and direct related program development and instruction.

Skills:

1. Skill in program development and instruction.

2. Skill in identifying trends in departments/programs and determining training impacts.

3. Skill in developing cost-effective programs and facilitating cutting-edge training methods used by up-to-date training specialists.

Abilities:

1. Ability to communicate effectively with all levels of employees; facilitate group processes and change.

2. Ability to develop/make effective presentations and serve as a trainer when qualified.

3. Ability to prioritize and coordinate multiple projects.

Equipment Operated: Standard office equipment including computers, fax machines, copiers, printers, telephones, etc.

Work Environment: Position is in a well-lighted office environment. Occasional evening and weekend work.

Mental/Physical Requirements: Involves sitting approximately 70 percent of the day, walking or standing the remainder and during training programs.

MARKETING

- Business Development Specialist
- Custom Service Specialist
- Marketing Communications Specialist
- Marketing Manager
- Marketing Representative
- Marketing Research Analyst

Business Development Specialist

Job Title:	Business Development Specialist
Department:	Marketing
Immediate Supervisor Title:	Marketing Manager
Job Supervisory Responsibilities:	None
General Summary:	An exempt, professional position responsible for establishing and maintaining referral relationships, developing contact lists of new referral sources, and acting as a liaison between referring physicians and the group practice.
Essential Job Responsibilities:	1. Establishes and maintains referral relationships.
	2. Maintains a database of physician contacts and referrals, tracking results and trends.
	3. Collaborates with the marketing manager to develop new marketing strategies and new business.
	4. Works with the marketing communications specialist to develop new marketing materials.
	5. Other duties as assigned.
Education:	Bachelor's degree in marketing, communications, or business administration.
Experience:	Minimum three years of experience in business development, preferably in the health care industry.
Other Requirements:	None

Performance Requirements: *Knowledge:*

1. Knowledge of computer database applications.

2. Knowledge of marketing/sales strategies.

Skills:

1. Skill in sales and attracting new customers.

2. Skill in effective oral and written communication.

Abilities:

1. Ability to develop and maintain effective relationships.

2. Ability to organize and analyze data.

3. Ability to utilize basic medical terminology.

Equipment Operated: Standard office equipment including computers, fax machines, copiers, printers, telephones, etc.

Work Environment: Position is in a well-lighted office environment. Occasional evening and weekend work.

Mental/Physical Requirements: Involves sitting approximately 90 percent of the day, walking or standing the remainder.

Customer Service Specialist

Job Title: Customer Service Specialist

Department: Marketing

Immediate Supervisor Title: Marketing Manager

Job Supervisory Responsibilities: None

General Summary: A nonexempt position responsible for responding to and following through on customer inquiries, issues, and concerns in a timely and accurate manner.

Essential Job Responsibilities:
1. Responds to telephone inquiries relating to the medical practice's policies and procedures.
2. Responds to written correspondence from customers.
3. Researches customer complaints/concerns and takes appropriate actions to resolve them.
4. Provides accurate information to customers regarding insurance benefits, providers, claims, referrals, eligibility, pharmaceuticals, etc.
5. Properly documents and files all customer complaints and results.
6. Other duties as assigned.

Education: High school diploma or equivalent. Some college is preferred.

Experience: Minimum three years of experience in customer service, preferably in the health care industry.

Other Requirements: None

Performance Requirements: *Knowledge:*

1. Knowledge of medical terminology.
2. Knowledge of insurance industry and billing procedures.
3. Knowledge of grammar, spelling, and punctuation for written and verbal correspondence.

Skills:

1. Skill in using computer programs and applications.
2. Skill in conflict resolution.

Abilities:

1. Ability to handle multiple priorities at the same time.
2. Ability to read, understand, and follow oral and written instruction.
3. Ability to communicate clearly and concisely.
4. Ability to establish effective working relationships with patients, employees, and the public.

Equipment Operated: Standard office equipment including computers, fax machines, copiers, printers, telephones, etc.

Work Environment: Position is in a well-lighted office environment. Occasional evening and weekend work.

Mental/Physical Requirements: Involves sitting approximately 90 percent of the day, walking or standing the remainder.

Marketing Communications Specialist

Job Title: Marketing Communications Specialist

Department: Marketing

Immediate Supervisor Title: Marketing Manager

Job Supervisory Responsibilities: None

General Summary: A nonexempt position responsible for communicating information related to the medical practice to various public groups including patients, referring physicians, payers, and the general public through multiple media, including print (brochures, advertisements, newsletters, press releases, etc.) and electronic (television, radio, Internet).

Essential Job Responsibilities:

1. Collaborates with marketing manager in the development of communications and publications goals to best educate public groups about the medical practice and to promote the practice.

2. Writes, designs, and coordinates placement and publication of ads, media announcements, marketing materials, publications.

3. Develops, designs, and coordinates new brochures and materials for clinical departments and/or refines existing materials, including physician directory.

4. Establishes and maintains positive relationships with local media. Coordinates interviews with media and appropriate medical practice managers.

5. Manages medical practice's Website according to organizational objectives including writing updates and coordinating with the Web master to post current information.

6. Other duties as assigned.

Education: Bachelor's degree in journalism, communications, or marketing.

Experience: Minimum three years of experience in communications, journalism, or marketing, preferably in the health care industry.

Other Requirements: None

Performance Requirements: *Knowledge:*

1. Knowledge of publication concepts including graphic design, layout, printing specifications, desktop publishing, and Web design.
2. Knowledge of interviewing, copywriting, editing, and other written and verbal communications concepts.

Skills:

1. Skill in designing and developing publications in their entirety, from concept through completion.
2. Skill in developing and implementing effective communications programs using writing and editing techniques and showing interpersonal, problem-solving, and decision-making competencies.

Abilities:

1. Ability to identify appropriate and newsworthy topics for publications and media relations.
2. Ability to write copy effectively for many different audiences using a computer.
3. Ability to develop creative, attractive designs using desktop and Web publishing and other graphics equipment.
4. Ability to work effectively with printers and other vendors to produce materials on time, to specification, and within budget.
5. Ability to coordinate and complete several tasks simultaneously.

Equipment Operated: Standard office equipment including computers, fax machines, copiers, printers, telephones, etc.

Work Environment: Position is in a well-lighted office environment. Occasional evening and weekend work. Vendor and media visits occasionally.

Mental/Physical Requirements: Involves sitting approximately 90 percent of the day, walking or standing the remainder.

Marketing Manager

Job Title:	Marketing Manager
Department:	Marketing
Immediate Supervisor Title:	Chief Executive Officer or Administrator
Job Supervisory Responsibilities:	Marketing Communications Specialist, Marketing Representative, Marketing Research Analyst, Business Development Specialist, Customer Service Specialist
General Summary:	An exempt, senior management position responsible for the development and direction of marketing and sales programs aligned with the clinic's strategic objectives and vision. Provides market analysis, develops strategies, and attracts new customers for all services. Develops and adheres to customer service goals. Enhances the medical practice through community outreach efforts and public relations.

Essential Job Responsibilities:

1. Establishes and achieves marketing goals to be met by the entire department.
2. Develops positive relations with major physicians and payers in the area.
3. Prepares payer-specific market analyses for administration.
4. Plans and directs programs to service all accounts.
5. Participates in the development of new products/services and strategies to maintain and enhance medical practice's position in the marketplace including customer satisfaction strategies.
6. Monitors, analyzes, and reports on the activities of competitors.

Education:	Bachelor's degree in business administration, marketing, communications, or health care. MBA or MS in marketing preferred.
Experience:	Minimum seven years of experience in health care promotion, marketing, or sales.
Other Requirements:	None

Performance Requirements: *Knowledge:*

1. Knowledge of marketing concepts including marketing strategies, competitive analysis, market research, product development, marketing communications, selling, public relations.

2. Knowledge of health care reimbursement, including all aspects of managed care payment practices.

Skills:

1. Skill in development of marketing strategies and marketing analyses.

2. Skill in sales and service management.

3. Skill in written and oral communications.

Abilities:

1. Ability to evaluate strategic marketing, pricing, and customer service issues.

2. Ability to coordinate multiple priorities.

3. Ability to strategically and tactically solve problems.

4. Ability to develop and maintain relationships with key internal and external stakeholders.

Equipment Operated: Standard office equipment including computers, fax machines, copiers, printers, telephones, etc.

Work Environment: Position is in a well-lighted office environment. Occasional evening and weekend work.

Mental/Physical Requirements: Involves sitting approximately 90 percent of the day, walking or standing the remainder.

Marketing Representative

Job Title:	Marketing Representative
Department:	Marketing
Immediate Supervisor Title:	Marketing Manager
Job Supervisory Responsibilities:	None
General Summary:	An exempt, sales position responsible for providing medical practice services to payers (insurance companies, health plans, employer groups) through personal selling activities, resulting in increase number of customers, contracts, and revenues. Acts as a liaison between current customers and the medical practice. Continually seeks additional referral sources.
Essential Job Responsibilities:	1. Arranges meetings with key representatives of payers to market the medical practice's services.
	2. Maintains and documents contact with payers to analyze needs and satisfaction.
	3. Reviews payer member profiles to identify potential for increasing volume of services provided by medical practice.
	4. Manages and maintains new and existing customer database by size, product, contact person, etc.
	5. Coordinates referrals for services.
	6. Other duties as assigned.
Education:	Bachelor's degree in marketing, business, or health administration.
Experience:	Minimum three years of sales experience in sales, marketing, public relations in the health care industry.
Other Requirements:	None

Performance Requirements: *Knowledge:*

1. Knowledge of concepts of marketing including market research, product development, marketing communications, selling, and public relations.
2. Knowledge of health care reimbursement, including all aspects of managed care payment practices and worker's compensation.

Skills:

1. Skill in developing and implementing marketing presentations.
2. Skill in developing and conducting needs analysis and satisfaction surveys.

Abilities:

1. Ability to read and interpret payer contracts.
2. Ability to organize and analyze information and present alternatives.
3. Ability to communicate effectively and respond positively to payers/customers as well as internal staff.
4. Ability to utilize basic medical and managed care terminology.

Equipment Operated: Standard office equipment including computers, fax machines, copiers, printers, telephones, etc.

Work Environment: Position is in a well-lighted office environment. Occasional evening and weekend work. Frequent visits to potential customers.

Mental/Physical Requirements: Involves sitting approximately 90 percent of the day, walking or standing the remainder.

Marketing Research Analyst

Job Title: Marketing Research Analyst

Department: Marketing

Immediate Supervisor Title: Marketing Manager

Job Supervisory Responsibilities: None

General Summary: A nonexempt position responsible for analyzing and communicating information to marketing, planning, finance, and administration to aid the process of management decision-making.

Essential Job Responsibilities:
1. Collects, inputs, and summarizes data for marketing reports and referral reports to track volumes and overall results.
2. Develops survey design techniques/coordinates the gathering and sharing of key data with other departments to aid in their decision-making.
3. Compiles marketing and planning data on competitors, referrals, patient origin, and volume to provide management and departments with data for internal and external analysis.
4. Collects marketing data from internal and external sources to provide management with up-to-date environmental assessment.
5. Updates/maintains database on physician referral data.
6. Other duties as assigned.

Education: Bachelor's degree in marketing or business administration.

Experience: Minimum three years of experience in market research, preferably with some experience in database management.

Other Requirements: None

Performance Requirements: *Knowledge:*

1. Knowledge of computer applications, including statistical packages and databases applications.
2. Knowledge of market competitive analysis as demonstrated through survey design and reports.
3. Knowledge of competitive intelligence as demonstrated through competitor research.

Skills:

1. Skill in development of survey design.
2. Skill in effective use of software.

Abilities:

1. Ability to be organized.
2. Ability to be self-motivated.
3. Ability to exercise independent judgment.

Equipment Operated: Standard office equipment including computers, fax machines, copiers, printers, telephones, etc.

Work Environment: Position is in a well-lighted office environment. Occasional evening and weekend work.

Mental/Physical Requirements: Involves sitting approximately 90 percent of the day, walking or standing the remainder.

INFORMATION TECHNOLOGY

- Chief Technology Officer
- Communications Specialist
- Computer Support Specialist
- Database Administrator
- IT Technical Assistant
- Program Analyst
- Web Master

Chief Technology Officer

Job Title: Chief Technology Officer

Department: Information Technology

Immediate Supervisor Title: Administrator or Office Manager

Job Supervisory Responsibilities: IT Technical Assistant, Computer Support Specialist, Communications Specialist, Program Analyst, Database Administrator, Web Master

General Summary: An exempt, management position responsible for planning, directing, developing, and maintaining the medical practice's information technology, including computers, computer networks and servers, computer programs, telecommunications, Website, and other technologies.

Essential Job Responsibilities:
1. Develops mission, plan, goals, policies, and budget for IT department.
2. Works with management team to identify strategic IT needs and establishes priorities for upgrades and modifications in line with clinic goals.
3. Develops, recommends, coordinates, and implements new or revised procedures, policies, programs, and equipment to ensure IT effectiveness.
4. Assists in correcting technical problems and issues as needed.
5. Ensures that computer hardware, including all computers, fax machines, printer, copiers, etc., function properly on a daily basis.
6. Develops and implements effective data backup and hardware security procedures and policies.

Education: Master's degree in computer science or information technology.

Experience: Minimum five years of experience in managing information technology in an office environment, preferably in the health care setting.

Other Requirements: None

Performance Requirements: *Knowledge:*

1. Knowledge of data analysis, systems design, problem identification, and medical data processing practice.

2. Knowledge of computer and server hardware, software, and data communications including comparability and system configuration.

3. Knowledge of basic programming languages.

4. Knowledge of fiscal management.

Skills:

1. Skill in using communication methods to elicit information, negotiate, resolve problems, and garner support.

2. Skill over a broad range of functional information technology management.

3. Skill in programming and project management if necessary to resolve critical problems, coordinate simultaneous efforts, recover from data loss, speed up development, and improve program efficiencies.

Abilities:

1. Ability to resolve conflicts productively.

2. Ability to separate problems into components and recognize underlying patterns and processes.

3. Ability to be oriented to end-user needs.

Equipment Operated: Standard office equipment including computers, fax machines, copiers, printers, telephones, etc.

Work Environment: Position is in a well-lighted office environment. Occasional evening and weekend work.

Mental/Physical Requirements: Involves sitting approximately 90 percent of the day, walking, bending, stretching, or standing the remainder. May require lifting up to 30 pounds.

Communications Specialist

Job Title:	Communications Specialist
Department:	Information Technology
Immediate Supervisor Title:	Chief Technology Officer
Job Supervisory Responsibilities:	None
General Summary:	A nonexempt position responsible for the medical practice's telecommunications system including telephone system, voicemail, and conference calling arrangements.

Essential Job Responsibilities:

1. Manages all telecommunications infrastructure including telephones, voice mail services, call forwarding options, conference calling, etc.
2. Develops and maintains policies and procedures regarding telephones. Trains new hires on the communication system.
3. Monitors and maintains the telecommunication system ensuring high performance.
4. Diagnoses and resolves problems within the system.
5. Troubleshoots and fixes employee's problems with phones and voice mail.
6. Other duties as assigned.

Education:	Bachelor's degree in Information Technology or related field.
Experience:	Minimum two years of experience maintaining telecommunication systems, preferably in the health care setting.
Other Requirements:	None

Performance Requirements:	*Knowledge:*
	1. Knowledge of telephones, voice lines, data lines, and voice mail.
	2. Knowledge of installation techniques of telecommunication systems.
	3. Knowledge of current trends in telecommunications.

Skills:

1. Skill in prioritizing tasks and project management.
2. Skill in using customer service skills in dealing with employees.
3. Skill in problem solving.

Abilities:

1. Ability to communicate effectively with all levels of employees.
2. Ability to a team player with effective interpersonal skills.
3. Ability to solve problems and work independently.

Equipment Operated: Standard office equipment including computers, fax machines, copiers, printers, telephones, etc.

Work Environment: Position is in a well-lighted office environment. Occasional evening and weekend work.

Mental/Physical Requirements: Involves sitting approximately 90 percent of the day, walking, bending, stretching, kneeling, or standing the remainder. May be required to lift up to 30 pounds.

Computer Support Specialist

Job Title:	Computer Support Specialist
Department:	Information Technology
Immediate Supervisor Title:	Chief Technology Officer
Job Supervisory Responsibilities:	None
General Summary:	A nonexempt position responsible for helping employees troubleshoot and fix computer-related problems.

Essential Job Responsibilities:

1. Provides all employees troubleshooting services and support for all operating system-, application-, program-, and hardware-related problems.
2. Works with the IT technical assistant to set up new computers.
3. Maintains functionality of all computers and printers.
4. Records and files all computer problems. Documents corrective actions taken.
5. Assists in computer program training.
6. Other duties as assigned.

Education:	High school diploma required; bachelor's degree preferred.
Experience:	Minimum two years of experience in computer support services, preferably in the health care industry.
Other Requirements:	None

Performance Requirements:	*Knowledge:*
	1. Extensive knowledge of computer programs and computer hardware.
	2. Knowledge of computer training principles and techniques.
	Skills:
	1. Skill in training variety of users on computer applications and programs.
	2. Skill in effective interpersonal skills and training methods.
	Abilities:
	1. Ability to clearly explain computer applications and programs in simple, user-friendly ways.
	2. Ability to effectively interact with all employees at all levels of computer understanding.
	3. Ability to be well organized and prioritize effectively.
Equipment Operated:	Standard office equipment including computers, fax machines, copiers, printers, telephones, etc.
Work Environment:	Position is in a well-lighted office environment. Occasional evening and weekend work.
Mental/Physical Requirements:	Involves sitting approximately 90 percent of the day, walking, kneeling, bending, or standing the remainder. May be required to lift up to 30 pounds.

Database Administrator

Job Title: Database Administrator

Department: Information Technology

Immediate Supervisor Title: Chief Technology Officer

Job Supervisory Responsibilities: None

General Summary: A nonexempt position responsible for developing, communicating, installing, and maintaining databases while ensuring high security and ease of data availability.

Essential Job Responsibilities:
1. Works with department directors and managers to develop policies and procedures regarding databases and security of data.
2. Ensures compliance with all database data and security of the data.
3. Develops procedures and policies to ensure high performance and ease of access for all users.
4. Designs and implements security and back-up systems for data recovery. Completes security audits to ensure that systems operate properly.
5. Other duties as assigned.

Education: Bachelor's degree in computer science, information technology, or related field.

Experience: Minimum five years of experience of database administration, preferably in the health care industry.

Other Requirements: None

Performance Requirements: *Knowledge:*

1. Knowledge of developing and building SQL databases.

2. Knowledge of data security and recovery techniques.

3. Knowledge of troubleshooting database problems.

Skills:

1. Skill in providing attention to detail and documentation.

2. Skill in both oral and written communication.

3. Skill in building effective working relationships.

Abilities:

1. Ability to communicate in a user-friendly, simple manner.

2. Ability to solve problems effectively.

3. Ability to be well organized and prioritize effectively.

Equipment Operated: Standard office equipment including computers, fax machines, copiers, printers, telephones, etc.

Work Environment: Position is in a well-lighted office environment. Occasional evening and weekend work.

Mental/Physical Requirements: Involves sitting approximately 90 percent of the day, walking or standing the remainder.

IT Technical Assistant

Job Title:	IT Technical Assistant
Department:	Information Technology
Immediate Supervisor Title:	Chief Technology Officer
Job Supervisory Responsibilities:	None
General Summary:	A nonexempt position responsible for providing technical assistance and support to all employees for computer hardware and software problems, troubleshooting, and training.
Essential Job Responsibilities:	1. Provides IT support and troubleshooting services to all employees.
	2. Performs and maintains IT security programs for all data, computer, and server hardware.
	3. Acts as the system administrator of all computer programs.
	4. Sets up and helps train new hires on computer hardware, software, and other equipment.
	5. Resolves all IT-related problems and keeps detailed records.
	6. Other duties as assigned.
Education:	Bachelor's degree in computer science or related field.
Experience:	Minimum two years of experience with IT support functions related to a wide variety of computer hardware, servers, and software, preferably in a health care sctting.
Other Requirements:	None

Performance Requirements: *Knowledge:*

1. Knowledge of operating systems, word processing, database applications, spreadsheet applications, e-mail applications, and diagnostic utilities.
2. Knowledge of troubleshooting and operating computer equipment.
3. Knowledge of customer service–related concepts.

Skills:

1. Skill in organizing tasks.
2. Skill in using customer service skills when dealing with frustrated employees.
3. Skill in masterful problem-solving.

Abilities:

1. Ability to communicate effectively in user-friendly terms both orally and in writing.
2. Ability to be a team player with effective interpersonal skills.
3. Ability to solve problems and work independently.

Equipment Operated: Standard office equipment including computers, fax machines, copiers, printers, telephones, etc.

Work Environment: Position is in a well-lighted office environment. Occasional evening and weekend work.

Mental/Physical Requirements: Involves sitting approximately 90 percent of the day, walking, bending, kneeling, stretching, or standing the remainder. May need to lift up to 30 pounds.

Program Analyst

Job Title:	Program Analyst
Department:	Information Technology
Immediate Supervisor Title:	Chief Technology Officer
Job Supervisory Responsibilities:	None
General Summary:	A nonexempt position responsible for system analysis, program design, coding, documentation, and other programming tasks.

Essential Job Responsibilities:

1. Programs custom applications to support the needs of the medical practice including extracting data from databases to satisfy standard ad hoc requests; developing databases, spreadsheets, and other programs to manipulate data.
2. Meets with users to gather system requirements, analyze the requirements, and formulate a plan to develop the systems and procedures to satisfy the requirements.
3. Provides basic training on software fundamental for new users on systems ensuring that all users are made aware of and trained on the use of new applications.
4. Maintains systems within the IT department to track and report user requests.
5. Performs analysis and testing on new software solutions prior to implementation.
6. Other duties as assigned.

Education:	Bachelor's degree in computer science, programming, or information technology.
Experience:	Minimum three years of experience in computer programming, preferably in a health care setting.
Other Requirements:	None

Performance Requirements:	*Knowledge:*
	1. Knowledge of major programming languages and operating systems.
	2. Knowledge of medical applications.

Skills:

1. Skill in developing application capabilities required in database, spreadsheet, and word processing.
2. Skill in maintaining safe operating environment.
3. Skill in using customer service techniques.

Abilities:

1. Ability to maintain strict confidentiality with patient data.
2. Ability to exercise professionalism when interacting with physicians, staff, and customers.
3. Ability to explain, both orally and in writing, technical topics in a clear and simple manner.

Equipment Operated: Standard office equipment including computers, fax machines, copiers, printers, telephones, etc.

Work Environment: Position is in a well-lighted office environment. Occasional evening and weekend work.

Mental/Physical Requirements: Involves sitting approximately 90 percent of the day, walking or standing the remainder.

Web Master

Job Title:	Web Master
Department:	Information Technology
Immediate Supervisor Title:	Chief Technology Officer
Job Supervisory Responsibilities:	None
General Summary:	A nonexempt position responsible for developing, designing, and maintaining the organization's Website.
Essential Job Responsibilities:	1. Designs, develops, and maintains an up-to-date Website.
	2. Ensures that the Website emulates the medical practice's image and vision.
	3. Writes comprehensive specifications and technical requirements for the Website.
	4. Diagnoses and resolves any hosting problems that create downtime for the Website.
	5. Ensures that security measures are effective and that privacy/confidentially policies are in compliance.
	6. Produces reports on Website statistics including number of hits, time spent on site, number of clicks, Google page rating, etc.
	7. Other duties as assigned.
Education:	Bachelor's degree in computer science, Web design, information technology, or related field.
Experience:	Minimum two years of experience in Web design, preferably as a Web master.
Other Requirements:	None

Performance Requirements: *Knowledge:*

1. Knowledge of Website design computer languages.

2. Knowledge of Web servers, Web hosting, and Website administration.

3. Knowledge of current trends in Websites and Internet, as well as online marketing.

Skills:

1. Skill in technical research, analysis, and detail orientation.

2. Skill in delivering technical projects on time, on budget, and to specifications.

3. Skill in programming, graphic design, and other Website-related computer applications and programs.

Abilities:

1. Ability to understand technical manuals, learn new techniques quickly, and adapt systems accordingly.

2. Ability to be effective as a team player and build a consensus within the IT department and with users and/or customers.

3. Ability to be a self-starter and take appropriate initiative.

Equipment Operated: Standard office equipment including computers, fax machines, copiers, printers, telephones, etc.

Work Environment: Position is in a well-lighted office environment. Occasional evening and weekend work.

Mental/Physical Requirements: Involves sitting approximately 90 percent of the day, walking or standing the remainder.

CLINICAL JOB DESCRIPTIONS

ALLIED HEALTH

- Certified Medical Assistant
- Clinical Staff Educator
- EEG Technician
- EKG Technician
- Phlebotomist
- Physician Assistant

Certified Medical Assistant

Job Title:	Certified Medical Assistant
Department:	Clinical Services
Immediate Supervisor Title:	Physician, Office Manager, Clinical Services Manager, or other designated medical personnel
Job Supervisory Responsibilities:	Certified medical assistants may assume the duties of the office manager with other staff to supervise and become the clinical manager of the physicians' back office and laboratory.
General Summary:	A nonexempt position responsible for performing a variety of duties depending on whether it is a small clinic, large medical practice, multi-clinic, or a specialty office. They may be involved in both the clinical and administrative areas including assisting physicians with patient care and handling clerical, environmental, and organizational tasks. Provides information to patients so they may fully utilize and benefit from the clinical services. May be assigned to specific medical specialty department (e.g., pediatrics).

Essential Job Responsibilities:

1. Fulfills patient care responsibilities as assigned that may include checking schedules and organizing patient flow; accompanying patients to exam/procedure room; assisting patients as needed with walking transfers, dressing, collecting specimens, preparing for exam, etc.; collecting patient history; performing screenings per provider guidelines; assisting physicians/nurses with various procedures; charting; relaying instructions to patients/families; answering calls, and providing pertinent information.

2. Fulfills clerical responsibilities as assigned that may include sending/receiving patient medical records; obtaining lab/X-ray reports, hospital notes, referral information, etc.; completing forms/requisitions as needed; scheduling appointments; verifying insurance coverage and patient demographics; managing and updating charts to ensure that information is complete and filed appropriately.

3. Fulfills environmental responsibilities as assigned that may include setting up instruments and equipment according to department protocols; cleaning exam/procedure rooms, instruments, and equipment between patient visits to maintain infection control; cleaning sterilizer according to scheduled maintenance program and keeping appropriate records; ordering, sorting, storing supplies; and restocking exam/procedure rooms.

4. Fulfills organizational responsibilities as assigned including respecting/promoting patient rights; responding appropriately to emergency codes; sharing problems relating to patients and/or staff with immediate supervisor.

5. Fulfills clinical medical assisting responsibilities that vary according to state law, which may include medical/surgical asepsis, sterilization, instrument wrapping and autoclaving; checking vital signs or mensurations; physical examination preparations; clinical pharmacology; drug administration through various routes including injections; prescription verifications with physician's orders; minor surgery assists including surgical tray set-up pre/post surgical care, applying dressings, and suture removal; biohazard waste disposal and monitoring; therapeutic modalities; instructing patients with assistive devices, body mechanics, and home care; laboratory procedures including Occupational Safety and Health Administration (OSHA) guidelines; quality control methods; CLIA-waived testing; capillary punctures and venipunctures; specimen handling such as urine, throat, vaginal, stool, and sputum; electrocardiography including mounting, emergency triage, and first aid. Medical assistants must adhere to the MA scope of practice in the laboratory.

6. Other duties as assigned.

Education: High school diploma or general equivalency diploma (GED), medical assistant diploma from an accredited vocational institution, or a community college course in medical assisting. Appropriate certificate indicating passing grade for specific specialty if working in specialty department; e.g., pediatric medical assistant exam.

Experience: Minimum one year of recent experience working in a medical facility as a medical assistant and/or documented evidence of externship completed in a medical office. Electrocardiogram (EKG), vital signs, venipuncture, capillary, and injection current experience.

Other Requirements: Current documentation of a national certification for the registered medical assistant (RMA) through the American Medical Technologists (AMT) or for the certified assistant through the American Association of Medical Assistants (AAMA). Must possess a current CPR certification and current health records with the appropriate immunizations to work in the health care field (hepatitis B and tuberculosis).

(continued on next page)

Certified Medical Assistant (continued)

Performance Requirements: *Knowledge:*

1. Knowledge of health care field and medical office protocols/procedures.
2. Knowledge of specific assisting tasks related to particular medical practice.
3. Knowledge of information that must be conveyed to patients and families.

Skills:

1. Skill in performing medical assistance tasks appropriately.
2. Skill in tact and diplomacy in interpersonal interactions.
3. Skill in understanding patient education needs by effectively sharing information with patients and families.

Abilities:

1. Ability to learn and retain information regarding patient care procedures.
2. Ability to project a pleasant and professional image.
3. Ability to plan, prioritize, and complete delegated tasks.
4. Ability to demonstrate compassion and caring in dealing with others.

Equipment Operated: Standard medical exam/office equipment, which may include computerized health information management system for medical records, etc.

Work Environment: Combination of medical office and exam/procedure room settings. Well-lighted, well-ventilated, adequate space.

Mental/Physical Requirements: Must be able to use appropriate body mechanics techniques when making necessary patient transfers and helping patients with walking, dressing, etc. Must be able to lift up to 30 pounds of supplies. Occasional stress from dealing with many staff and patients.

Clinical Staff Educator

Job Title:	Clinical Staff Educator
Department:	Clinical Services
Immediate Supervisor Title:	Clinical Services Manager
Job Supervisory Responsibilities:	None
General Summary:	An exempt position responsible for creating, designing, implementing, and continually improving training programs for nurses and allied health clinicians.

Essential Job Responsibilities:

1. Participates in strategic planning with clinical services manager and other senior staff to identify trends in clinical care and related future training.
2. Conducts training needs analysis to gather information and target future training opportunities. Evaluates current programs for relevance and successful outcomes.
3. Designs and develops curricula and clinical educational programs to meet needs.
4. Provides expert advice and counsel to internal customers regarding education and training.
5. Presents variety of clinical training programs. Conducts train-the-trainer sessions to enable others to teach these programs.
6. Identifies and evaluates off-site educational programs including management and skills training for staff. Coordinates, schedules, and documents vendor training.
7. Other duties as assigned.

Education:	BSN or other clinical degree. MS in instructional design and adult learning preferred.
Experience:	Minimum five years of experience as clinician, plus three to five years experience as clinical staff trainer.
Other Requirements:	Current RN state license or other license/certification related to clinical specialty. Current CPR certificate.

Performance Requirements: *Knowledge:*

1. Knowledge of techniques and strategies for conducting educational program needs assessment.
2. Knowledge of quality improvement principles.
3. Knowledge of adult learning theories and techniques.

Skills:

1. Skill in problem-solving and analysis.
2. Skill in team building.
3. Skill in conflict resolution.

Abilities:

1. Ability to present programs effectively to other clinicians.
2. Ability to teach others to present the programs proficiently.
3. Ability to interact with variety of clinicians in user-friendly manner.

Equipment Operated: Standard office and training equipment including computers and audio-visual machines.

Work Environment: Mostly classroom and medical office environment. Little contact with patients.

Mental/Physical Requirements: Primarily sedentary. May spend two to six hours per day standing during program presentations. May lift/carry equipment weighing up to 50 pounds. May create stress if dealing with tight deadlines related to training.

EEG Technician

Job Title: EEG Technician

Department: Clinical Services

Immediate Supervisor Title: Clinical Services Manager

Job Supervisory Responsibilities: None

General Summary: A nonexempt position responsible for assisting with electroencephalographs (EEG), an instrument that measures and records the electric activity of the brain, and related patient care.

Essential Job Responsibilities:

1. Obtains patient history, including concerns and habits. Gets sedation order from physician when needed.
2. Explains EEG procedure and preparation to patient and makes him/her as comfortable as possible. Uses patient education materials as applicable.
3. Applies and fills electrodes. Takes EEG, produces EEG/graphic records. Records EEG results. Removes electrodes.
4. Tells patient when/where results will be shared.
5. Orders supplies such as collodion, electrodes, acetone, EEG paper, ink, and pens. Cleans/maintains equipment, initiates maintenance repairs.
6. Establishes safety check system for all EEG equipment, including any at satellite sites.
7. Completes paperwork, including charge slips for EEG. Documents information in medical record. Maintains EEG files. Maintains complete records on all normal and abnormal EEGs for time periods established by protocol.
8. Other duties as assigned.

Education: High school diploma. Completion of accredited EEG training program.

Experience: Minimum one year of experience as EEG technician, preferably in clinic setting.

Other Requirements: None

Performance Requirements: *Knowledge:*

1. Knowledge of EEG technology, principles, and methods.
2. Knowledge of how to use EEG and related equipment in clean, safe manner.
3. Knowledge of customer service principles.

Skills:

1. Skill in using EEG concepts to provide effective assistance to clinical team.
2. Skill in using EEG equipment in line with safety, infection control, and quality assurance protocols.
3. Skill in demonstrating customer service philosophy through effective patient education.

Abilities:

1. Ability to interact effectively with all members of the clinical team.
2. Ability to organize and prioritize tasks effectively.
3. Ability to complete paperwork accurately and in timely manner.

Equipment Operated: Standard EEG equipment including machines, collodian, electrodes, acetone, EEG paper, ink, and pens. Computer hardware/software for documentation.

Work Environment: Exam room and medical office setting. Frequent contact with diverse individuals. Exposure to communicable diseases and other conditions common in clinic setting.

Mental/Physical Requirements: Requires standing six to eight hours per day. Must be able to lift/carry/move 75 pounds of equipment. Occasionally assist with patient transfer/transport. Some stress when dealing with anxious patients.

EKG Technician

Job Title:	EKG Technician
Department:	Clinical Services or Laboratory
Immediate Supervisor Title:	Clinical Services Manager or Laboratory Manager
Job Supervisory Responsibilities:	None
General Summary:	A nonexempt position responsible for assisting with diagnostic tests using electrocardiograms (EKGs) to capture patient heart rhythm and rate. (EKGs are performed before/after operations, during physicals, examinations of patients with a history of heart disease, when patients are experiencing chest pains, and other times deemed necessary by physicians.)

Essential Job Responsibilities:

1. Explains EKG procedure and testing preparation to patients using patient-appropriate materials. May record additional medical history. Prepares patients for Holter monitor use. Assists physician with stress tests and other procedures.

2. Performs tests under physician direction on patients in caring and competent manner, monitoring blood pressure and heart rate during procedure.

3. Explains to patient when/how results will be available.

4. Completes necessary documentation including EKG log. Documents patient information in medical record. Maintains EKG files.

5. Orders supplies and equipment for department. Cleans/maintains equipment and initiates repairs. Cleans/stocks exam rooms based on safety and injection control procedures.

6. Other duties as assigned.

Education:	High school diploma. Successful completion of EKG course from accredited program including clinical externship.
Experience:	Minimum one year of experience preferred. On-the-job training may be available for nursing aides and others with health care experience.
Other Requirements:	None

Performance Requirements: *Knowledge:*

1. Knowledge of EKG principles, methods, and tests. Stays current with state-of-the-art procedures.
2. Knowledge of proper usage of EKG equipment, Holter monitor, and other equipment in the department.
3. Knowledge of safety, infection control, and quality assurance protocols.

Skills:

1. Skill in using customer services concepts including appropriately teaching patients about procedures.
2. Skill in performing EKG and other tests.
3. Skill in documentation including use of computer.

Abilities:

1. Ability to put patients at ease using pleasant, relaxed manner.
2. Ability to organize time and prioritize work appropriately.
3. Ability to communicate effectively via correct documentation.

Equipment Operated: EKG equipment, Holter monitor, and other instruments used in testing.

Work Environment: May encounter stressful working conditions related to close contact with patients with serious heart conditions and/or with possible life-or-death complications and implications. Frequent exposure to communicable diseases and other conditions common in clinic setting.

Mental/Physical Requirements: Considerable time spent walking and standing for up to four to six hours per day. Heavy lifting of 75+ pounds may be involved to move equipment or transfer. Some stress related to dealing with anxious patients.

Phlebotomist

Job Title:	Phlebotomist
Department:	Laboratory
Immediate Supervisor Title:	Laboratory Manager, Physician, or other designated medical personnel.
Job Supervisory Responsibilities:	None
General Summary:	A nonexempt position responsible for performing venipuncture on patients.

Essential Job Responsibilities:

1. Prepares equipment to efficiently collect blood products.
2. Performs venipuncture, arterial and capillary punctures on patients as directed by physician and following medical practice protocols related to safety, infection control, and confidentiality. Conducts laboratory tests on specimens. Enters data into computer.
3. Assists donor before, during, and after donation. Instructs on urine collection procedures.
4. Cleans/sterilizes equipment, instruments, and work area following safety, cleanliness, and infection control procedures.
5. Inventories supplies and places orders to ensure adequate supplies for procedures.

Education: High school diploma or equivalent. Graduation from an accredited medical vocational institution with phlebotomy course diploma.

Experience: Minimum one year of phlebotomy experience. Medical practice experience helpful.

Other Requirements: ASCP required; certification as medical assistant preferred but not required. National certification through American Medical Technologists as a registered phlebotomy technician not required but helpful. Current CPR certificate.

Performance Requirements: *Knowledge:*

1. Knowledge of phlebotomy techniques.

2. Knowledge of clinic protocols and policies.

Skills:

1. Skill in performing efficient and effective draws.

2. Skill in conducting cooperative interactions with patients and staff.

Abilities:

1. Ability to interpret and respond appropriately to instructions.

2. Ability to coordinate eye–hand movements to ensure patient comfort during blood draws.

Equipment Operated: Blood draw equipment including syringes, tubes, bandages, and other appropriate supplies.

Work Environment: Performs duties in medical exam/procedure rooms. Exposure to communicable diseases, sharp instruments, bodily fluids, cleaning chemicals.

Mental/Physical Requirements: Involves standing six to eight hours per day, walking, bending, and reaching. Must be able to lift up to 30 pounds of supplies and equipment and help with patient transport and transfer. Occasional stress when dealing with priorities and anxious patients.

Physician Assistant

Job Title:	Physician Assistant
Department:	Clinical Services
Immediate Supervisor Title:	Clinical Services Manager and Physicians
Job Supervisory Responsibilities:	None
General Summary:	An exempt position responsible for practicing medicine with physician supervision including conducting examinations and writing prescriptions. Within physician–physician assistant (PA) relationship, PAs exercise autonomy in medical decision making and provide a broad range of diagnostic and therapeutic services. May practice in several primary care areas including family medicine, internal medicine, pediatrics, and obstetrics/gynecology as well as surgery and surgical subspecialties. May include responsibility for education, research, and administrative services.

Essential Job Responsibilities:

1. Conducts physical exams, assesses health status, orders and interprets tests, prescribes medications, and treats illnesses including giving injections and suturing wounds. Consults with physicians as needed and refers to physicians for more complicated medical cases or cases that are not a routine part of a PA's scope of work.

2. Monitors therapies and provides continuity of care.

3. Triages patient calls and evaluates patient problems. Responds to emergencies including use of CPR.

4. Counsels patient/family on preventive health care.

5. Documents patient information and care in medical record and may maintain department statistical database for research purposes.

Education:	Bachelor's degree and successful completion of accredited physician assistant program.
Experience:	Four years of health care experience prior to applying to PA program, plus one year of experience as PA, preferably in clinic setting.
Other Requirements:	National certification from the National Commission on Certification of PAs. To maintain their national certification, PAs must log 100 hours of continuing medical education every two years and sit for a recertification every six years. State PA license also required. Current CPR certificate required.

Performance Requirements: *Knowledge:*

1. Knowledge of medical model and roles of physicians and physician assistants. Familiar with anatomy, pharmacology, pathophysiology, clinical medicine, and physical diagnosis.

2. Knowledge of patient assessment techniques including taking medical histories, performing physicals, evaluating health status including state of wellness, and compliance with care recommendations.

3. Knowledge of diagnosing and treating medical problems and developing care plans.

4. Knowledge of documentation in medical records in confidential manner.

Skills:

1. Skill in gathering and analyzing physiological, socioeconomic, and emotional patient data.

2. Skill in accurately evaluating patient problems in person or via phone and providing appropriate advice, intervention, or referral.

3. Skill in developing/revising patient care plan based on patient status.

Abilities:

1. Ability to make responsible decisions within scope of PA practice.

2. Ability to collaborate effectively with physicians on complicated cases.

3. Ability to educate patients, families, and staff in user-friendly manner.

4. Ability to demonstrate eye–hand coordination, full range of motion, and manual dexterity.

Equipment Operated: Medical instruments required for physical exams and minor surgery and computer hardware/software.

Work Environment: Medical office and exam room settings. Frequent exposure to communicable diseases, biohazards, and other conditions common to clinic. Frequent contact with variety of people.

Mental/Physical Requirements: Involves standing, sitting, walking, bending, stooping, and twisting. May be required to help to transfer patient. High level of responsibility and heavy workload can generate stress.

CLINICAL SUPPORT STAFF

- Appointment Manager
- Appointment Scheduler
- Medical Administrative Assistant

Appointment Manager

Job Title: Appointment Manager

Department: Clinical Services

Immediate Supervisor Title: Clinical Services Manager

Job Supervisory Responsibilities: Appointment Schedulers

General Summary: An exempt position responsible for providing supervision to appointment schedulers and serving as back-up support. Works closely with clinical managers and physicians to ensure physician/clinician and patient appointment preferences are met.

Essential Job Responsibilities:

1. Supervises appointment schedulers, including participating in their hiring, training, and evaluation, to ensure the most efficient matching of physician/clinician availability and patient preferences for time and date.
2. Assumes role of appointment scheduler when scheduler is ill or on vacation.
3. Collaborates with information technology department on maintaining and upgrading the computerized scheduling system.
4. Works with clinical services manager and physicians/clinicians to ensure scheduling procedures are meeting needs.
5. Acts as resource for appointment schedulers when they encounter patient issues such as customer complaints or physician dissatisfaction with appointments.
6. Produces reports on appointment patterns, trends, complaints, and outcomes and analyzes results. Makes recommendations about improvement opportunities.
7. Other duties as assigned.

Education: High school diploma; associate's degree preferred.

Experience: Minimum three to five years of scheduling experience, with one year of experience in a clinical setting, preferably a medical practice.

Other Requirements: None

Performance Requirements: *Knowledge:*

1. Knowledge of medical practice protocols related to appointment scheduling.

2. Knowledge of medical terminology for interpreting physician instructions and patient needs.

3. Knowledge of confidentiality requirements related to patient information.

Skills:

1. Skill in training new appointment schedulers about medical practice scheduling system.

2. Skill in evaluating scheduler performance and correcting performance deviations.

3. Skill in serving as resource to schedulers with questions or issues and about the computerized system.

Abilities:

1. Ability to communicate instructions clearly.

2. Ability to collaborate with all levels of clinicians and staff to meet needs.

3. Ability to analyze data reports and make recommendations for improvement.

Equipment Operated: Standard office equipment with emphasis on telephone and computer hardware/software.

Work Environment: Medical office, well lighted, well ventilated. Rare contact with patients.

Mental/Physical Requirements: Mostly sedentary. Some walking, bending, and reaching. Repetitive use of computer may lead to nerve damage without ergonomic measures. Occasional stress from dealing with patients with appointment issues.

Appointment Scheduler

Job Title: Appointment Scheduler

Department: Clinical Services

Immediate Supervisor Title: Appointment Manager

Job Supervisory Responsibilities: None

General Summary: A nonexempt position responsible for making appointments for patients following medical practice procedures. Tasks may be integrated into another position, e.g., receptionist/registration clerk or medical assistant.

Essential Job Responsibilities:

1. Schedules appointments for patients either by phone when they call in or in person after an office visit. If medical practice offers after-hours/one-day appointments, schedules these appointments following urgent/emergency protocols as in the case of a sick child, which may mean scheduling the patient with a physician or nurse practitioner other than their primary physician.

2. Uses manual/computerized system to match physician/clinician availability with patient's preferences in terms of date and time.

3. Maintains scheduling system so records are accurate and complete and can be used to analyze patient/staffing patterns. Provides daily schedules to physicians/clinicians or medical assistants prior to each day's visits. Copies also made available to the receptionist/registration clerk and others as needed.

4. Ensures that updates (e.g., cancellations or additions) are input daily into master schedule.

5. Communicates as needed with physicians/clinicians and other staff about any patient concerns/issues related to scheduling. Consults with appointment manager about any system problems.

6. Uses customer service principles and techniques to deal with patients calmly and pleasantly.

7. Other duties as assigned.

Education: High school diploma.

Experience: Minimum one year of experience in an appointment scheduling position, preferably in a medical practice setting.

Other Requirements: None

Performance Requirements: *Knowledge:*

1. Knowledge of medical practice protocols related to scheduling appointments.
2. Knowledge of manual/computerized scheduling systems.
3. Knowledge of customer service principles and techniques.

Skills:

1. Skill in communicating effectively with physicians/clinicians about scheduling preferences.
2. Skill in maintaining master appointment schedule via manual or computerized means.
3. Skill in producing reports about appointment patterns as needed.

Abilities:

1. Ability to multitask effectively, dealing with phone calls, in-office patients, staff, and others pleasantly.
2. Ability to communicate calmly and clearly with patients about appointments in all circumstances including when they are ill or have an emergency.
3. Ability to analyze situations and respond appropriately.

Equipment Operated: Standard office equipment with emphasis on computer hardware and software as well as telephone.

Work Environment: Medical office or reception area. Exposure to communicable diseases and other conditions related to clinic setting.

Mental/Physical Requirements: Mostly sedentary with some standing, walking, reaching. Daily and repetitive data entry may cause nerve problems unless ergonomic techniques are used. Periodic stress from handling many calls and patient requests.

Medical Administrative Assistant

Job Title:	Medical Administrative Assistant
Department:	Clinical Services
Immediate Supervisor Title:	Office Manager, Clinical Services Manager, Physician, or other designated supervisor
Job Supervisory Responsibilities:	None
General Summary:	A nonexempt position responsible for performing a variety of clerical duties for office manager, clinical services manager, or physicians.

Essential Job Responsibilities:

1. Greets, screens, schedules, and directs patients to exam rooms.
2. Performs clerical duties related to clinical services including medical transcription, composition, and dictation in a medical group.
3. Prepares and processes correspondence. Answers routine medical administrative inquiries and drafts letters for physicians and other clinical staff.
4. Performs medical receptionist duties as necessary. Answers telephone, screens calls, takes messages, and provides information.
5. Obtains, verifies, and updates patient information and provides support services to patients and medical staff.
6. Requests, locates, sends, and receives patient medical records.
7. Maintains medical appointment books for patients, meetings, travel, etc. Arranges meetings for clinical staff.
8. Prepares clinical services organizational charts and timetables. Assists with preparation of agendas, materials, notes, etc.
9. Attends meetings, takes and distributes minutes.
10. Maintains files and assists in establishing office systems.
11. Orders office and clinical supplies. Assists in the care and maintenance of office equipment.

Education:	High school diploma or general equivalency diploma (GED). Diploma as a medical administrative assistant from an accredited medical vocational course preferred.
Experience:	Minimum two years of administrative assistant experience in a medical office setting.
Other Requirements:	Medical administrative specialist certification preferred from American Medical Technologists.

Performance Requirements: *Knowledge:*

1. Knowledge of medical terminology and office procedures.

2. Knowledge of grammar, spelling, and punctuation to type from draft copy and review and edit reports and correspondence.

3. Knowledge of basic arithmetic to make calculations, balance and reconcile figures, and make changes accurately.

Skills:

1. Skill in operating office equipment.

2. Skill in organizational matters, including time management, prioritization, multitasking, and problem-solving.

Abilities:

1. Ability to type 60 words per minute using word-processing software. Able to learn/use other computer programs including Microsoft® Excel, e-mail, Internet, and Microsoft® PowerPoint.

2. Ability to read, understand, and follow oral and written instructions.

3. Ability to sort and file materials correctly using alphabetic or numeric systems.

4. Ability to communicate clearly and concisely.

5. Ability to establish and maintain effective working relationships with patients, physicians and other clinical staff, and the public.

Equipment Operated: Office machinery including computers, fax, dictating machine, calculator, and photocopier.

Work Environment: Work performed in office environment. Involves frequent contact with staff and patients.

Mental/Physical Requirements: Manual dexterity for office machine operation including computer and calculator; stooping, bending to handle files and supplies, mobility to complete errands or deliveries, or sitting for extended periods of time. Stress can be triggered by multiple staff demands and deadlines.

HEALTH INFORMATION MANAGEMENT/MEDICAL RECORDS

- Medical Records/Health Information Technician
- Medical Transcriptionist

Medical Records/Health Information Technician

Job Title: Medical Records/Health Information Technician

Department: Medical Records, Health Information

Immediate Supervisor Title: Medical Records, Health Information, or Clinical Services Manager

Job Supervisory Responsibilities: None

General Summary: A nonexempt position responsible for assembling patient information into patients' medical charts/records in accurate and complete manner. Position responsibilities vary by size of medical practice and type of technology used such as electronic medical records versus manual files.

Essential Job Responsibilities:

1. Assembles patients' health information including patient symptoms and medical history, exam results, X-ray reports, lab tests, diagnoses, and treatment plans. Checks to ensure all forms are completed, properly identified, and signed and that all necessary information is in the manual and/or computer file in preferred manner such as chronological.

2. Communicates as needed with physicians and other health care professionals to clarify diagnoses or to obtain additional information.

3. Submits files/documentation to physicians and other clinicians as requested for review, quality assurance checks, and other purposes.

4. Provides charts/documents requested for use in legal actions, following patient consent/confidentiality protocols.

5. Codes patients' information periodically (as back-up) for insurance purposes. Assigns a code to each diagnosis and procedure (diagnosis-related group [DRG]).

6. Uses computer programs if requested to tabulate and analyze data to improve patient care, control costs, respond to surveys, or use in research studies.

7. Other duties as assigned.

Education: High school diploma. Associate's degree from a community/junior college preferred.

Experience: Minimum two years of medical records clerk/health information technician experience, preferably in medical practice setting.

Other Requirements: Registered health information technician (RHIT) designation preferred, but not required. Offered by the American Health Information Management Association; designation awarded after successfully completing written exam.

Performance Requirements:	*Knowledge:*

Knowledge:

1. Knowledge of biology, chemistry, health, and computer science.
2. Knowledge of medical terminology.
3. Knowledge of legal and ethical considerations related to patient information.

Skills:

1. Skill in putting information in preferred medical record system, meeting clinic standards.
2. Skill in dealing with masses of information in organized manner.
3. Skill in using computer and medical records software.

Abilities:

1. Ability to alphabetize and put information (materials, forms, etc.) into chronological order.
2. Ability to analyze medical records for completeness and accuracy, paying attention to detail.
3. Ability to schedule time and assignments effectively.

Equipment Operated: Range of medical records equipment and supplies, including computer hardware/software, manual files, and sorters.

Work Environment: Usually pleasant and comfortable offices. Little contact with patients.

Mental/Physical Requirements: Combination of standing, sitting, bending, and reaching. May work at computer monitors for prolonged periods with danger of eye strain and muscle pain. Stress generated if workload is heavy.

Medical Transcriptionist

Job Title:	Medical Transcriptionist
Department:	Health Information/Medical Records or Clinical Services
Immediate Supervisor Title:	Health Information/Medical Records Manager or Clinical Services Manager
Job Supervisory Responsibilities:	None

General Summary: A nonexempt position responsible for transcribing dictated recordings made by physicians and other health care professionals into medical reports, correspondence, and other administrative material, which typically become part of patients' permanent files. Often this task is outsourced to contract transcription companies. Sometimes this task is handled by employees working at home via telecommuting techniques.

Essential Job Responsibilities:

1. Listens to dictated recordings via headset if using traditional digital or analog equipment (see Equipment Operated section for equipment options).
2. Transcribes dictation, using a foot pedal to pause the recording when necessary if using traditional equipment. Keys the text into a personal computer or word processor.
3. Edits as necessary for grammar and clarity.
4. Produces a variety of documents, including discharge summaries, history and physical examination reports, operative reports, consultation reports, autopsy reports, diagnostic imaging studies, progress notes, and referral letters.
5. Returns transcribed documents to the physicians or other health care professionals for review and signature or correction.
6. Other duties as assigned such as receiving patients, scheduling appointments, answering the telephone, and handling mail.

Education: High school diploma. Completion of a two-year associate's degree or one-year certificate (certified medical transcriptionist [CMT]) program is recommended, but not always required. On-the-job training often available in a medical practice supervised by an experienced transcriptionist.

Experience: Minimum two years of medical transcription experience, preferably in a medical practice environment.

Other Requirements: CMT voluntary designation preferred from the American Association for Medical Transcription, awarded to those who earn a passing score on a certification examination. Continuing education credits required every three years for renewal.

Performance Requirements: *Knowledge:*

1. Knowledge of medical terminology, anatomy and physiology, diagnostic procedures, pharmacology, and treatment assessments.
2. Knowledge of how to translate medical jargon and abbreviations into their expanded forms using electronic and printed medical reference materials.
3. Knowledge of medical record protocols and legal and ethical requirements related to keeping patient information confidential.

Skills:

1. Skill in spotting mistakes or inconsistencies in a medical report and checking to correct the information.
2. Skill in following medical record style standards.
3. Skill in keeping up-to-date with medical field changes.

Abilities:

1. Ability to understand and question patient assessment and treatment notes to reduce the chance of patients receiving ineffective or even harmful treatments. Ensures high-quality care.
2. Ability to stay current with medical transcription equipment as the technology changes through ongoing research and education.
3. Ability to communicate effectively with physicians and other health care professionals related to transcription questions and concerns.

Equipment Operated: Wide range of equipment that changes rapidly because of technology evolution. Ranges from digital/analog dictating equipment with headsets and foot pedals, to dictation received over the Internet with a quick return of transcribed documents to clients for approval, to speech recognition technology, which electronically translates sound into text and creates drafts of reports. These are then formatted; edited for mistakes in translation, punctuation, or grammar; and checked for consistency and any possible medical errors.

Work Environment: Comfortable setting in office or in own home. Many transcriptionists telecommute from home-based offices as employees or subcontractors for transcription services or as self-employed independent contractors.

Mental/Physical Requirements: Hazards related to sitting in the same position for long periods. Can suffer wrist, back, neck, or eye problems due to strain and risk repetitive motion injuries such as carpal tunnel syndrome. Constant pressure to be accurate and productive can be stressful.

LABORATORY/RADIOLOGY

- Laboratory Manager
- Laboratory Technician
- Mammographer/Mammography Technologist
- Nuclear Medicine Technologist
- Radiation Therapist
- Sonographer/Ultrasonographer
- X-Ray Technician

Laboratory Manager

Job Title: Laboratory Manager

Department: Laboratory

Immediate Supervisor Title: Clinical Services Manager

Job Supervisory Responsibilities: Laboratory Assistants and Laboratory Technicians; may supervise phlebotomist

General Summary: An exempt position responsible for planning, directing, and supervising a laboratory operation. Also conducts and interprets complex microbiological tests.

Essential Job Responsibilities:
1. Conducts purchasing, budget-tracking, and inventory management for the laboratory.
2. Manages activities of assigned staff. Oversees or conducts training and new employee orientation. Manages workload and scheduling. Responds to grievances of patients as well as employee-related issues. Handles performance management issues and participates in hiring.
3. Ensures maintenance of laboratory instruments and equipment. Oversees quality assurance procedures. Ensures adequate safety and compliance with standard operating procedures. Requests new equipment as needed and develops new laboratory procedures.
4. Performs microbiological laboratory testing and interprets findings in assigned specialty areas.
5. Measures and monitors key performance areas of laboratory. Recommends ways to promote continuous quality improvement, customer service, and employee satisfaction.
6. Other duties as assigned.

Education: Bachelor's degree, preferably in microbiology, medical technology, or health sciences. Master's degree in health administration preferred.

Experience: Minimum five years of experience in progressively responsible positions in laboratory, including two years supervisory experience.

Other Requirements: American Medical Technologist certification.

Performance Requirements: *Knowledge:*

1. Knowledge of principles and techniques of clinical laboratory testing procedures/practices and of microbiology, including medical mycology; mycobacteriology; enteric, sexually transmitted and environmental bacteriology, parasitology and virology.

2. Knowledge of medical terminology, communicable diseases, and environmental health issues.

3. Knowledge of laboratory regulations, including quality control of media and reagents, laboratory safety, laboratory documentation requirements, sterilization requirements, and laboratory equipment.

4. Knowledge of applicable microbiological testing techniques, including tests for AIDS, rubella, hepatitis, and syphilis.

5. Knowledge of planning, budgeting, quality control, customer service, and supervision.

Skills:

1. Skill in performing laboratory tests.

2. Skill in project planning, laboratory operations, and budgetary control.

3. Skill in using computers for database management, testing, and record-keeping functions.

Abilities:

1. Ability to communicate appropriately, both orally and written.

2. Ability to collaborate effectively with health care team.

3. Ability to recognize and resolve hazardous conditions. Able to deal calmly with emergency situations.

4. Ability to perform mathematical calculations.

5. Ability to demonstrate full range of motion, manual dexterity, and eye–hand coordination in use of equipment and instruments.

Equipment Operated: Standard laboratory equipment including various testing instruments.

Work Environment: Combination of laboratory and office settings. Exposure to communicable diseases, biohazards, toxic substances, and other conditions common in clinical laboratory environment.

Mental/Physical Requirements: Varied activities including sitting, standing, walking, bending, lifting, and reaching. Frequent standing and working for extended periods of time. Periodic need to lift and carry items weighing up to 50 pounds. Some stress related to ensuring accuracy and safety of operation.

Laboratory Technician

Job Title:	Laboratory Technician
Department:	Laboratory
Immediate Supervisor Title:	Laboratory Manager
Job Supervisory Responsibilities:	May participate in supervision of laboratory assistants
General Summary:	A nonexempt position responsible for providing technical support for laboratory operations.

Essential Job Responsibilities:

1. Performs technical laboratory functions including chemistry, hematology, urinalysis, immunology, allergy testing, and other tests. Performs echocardiography (EKG), phlebotomy, pulmonary function testing tasks on occasion.

2. Reports test results following clinic protocols, alerting physicians and/or nurses immediately about "red flag" results.

3. Ensures quality control in collecting specimens and in ensuring appropriate sampling and record keeping. May instruct laboratory assistant on housekeeping and other tasks.

4. Maintains equipment, instruments, and supplies as needed.

5. Complies with all quality assurance policies and Occupational Safety and Health Administration (OSHA) regulations related to safety, cleanliness, and infection control.

6. Other duties as assigned.

Education:	High school diploma. Successful completion of medical technologist, medical laboratory technician, or certified laboratory assistant program.
Experience:	Minimum two years of laboratory experience, preferably in clinic setting.
Other Requirements:	American Medical Technologist certification.

Performance Requirements: *Knowledge:*

1. Knowledge of medical laboratory principles, standards, applications, and tests.
2. Knowledge of use and maintenance of laboratory equipment and instruments.
3. Knowledge of safety, infection control, and quality assurance policies and regulations.

Skills:

1. Skill in applying appropriate testing procedures.
2. Skill in equipment proper use, preventive maintenance, and repair.
3. Skill in appropriate quality control and confidentiality procedures.

Abilities:

1. Ability to exercise independent judgment, problem solve, make decisions, and use discretion in reporting/distributing results.
2. Ability to establish and maintain cooperative relationships with patients, families, and staff.
3. Ability to organize workload effectively and work quickly with high level of accuracy using manual/finger dexterity and eye–hand coordination.

Equipment Operated: Standard laboratory equipment and instrumentation.

Work Environment: Laboratory unit, well lighted and temperature controlled. Exposure to chemicals, communicable diseases, biohazards, and other conditions related to medical setting.

Mental/Physical Requirements: Varied activities including standing, walking, sitting, bending, reaching, lifting, and stooping. May occasionally need to lift/carry 50 pounds. Some stress related to ensuring accuracy of work.

Mammographer/Mammography Technologist

Job Title:	Mammographer/Mammography Technologist
Department:	Radiology, Women's Health or Clinical Services
Immediate Supervisor Title:	Department Manager
Job Supervisory Responsibilities:	None
General Summary:	A nonexempt position responsible for screening and diagnostic exams of the breast, aiding in the early detection of breast cancer.

Essential Job Responsibilities:

1. Collaborates with radiologist to consider many factors related to breast imaging to ensure unit is operating in clinically safe and effective manner.
2. Explains procedure to patients, including dressing in a gown before the process.
3. Adjusts equipment, positions patient, and provides adequate radiation protection. Selects length and intensity for radiation exposure on an individual basis.
4. Compresses breasts appropriately to get clear images.
5. Develops radiologic film and examines for technical quality and diagnostic acceptability.
6. Delivers film to radiologist for reading/interpretation immediately or at a later time.
7. Releases patient upon completion of exam. Discusses results or explains how results will be shared later.
8. Other duties as assigned.

Education: High school diploma. Successful completion of an accredited course in radiologic technology or associate degree in radiologic technology. Must have a minimum of 28 classroom hours for initial mammographer training as designated by the Mammography Quality Standards Act (MQSA).

Experience: Minimum two years of experience in radiology imaging modalities; one year mammography experience preferred in medical practice setting.

Other Requirements: Current certification with the American Registry of Radiologic Technologists. Current state permit/license as general diagnostic radiographer.

Performance Requirements: *Knowledge:*

1. Knowledge of anatomy, breast physiology, breast abnormalities, and clinical breast exams.

2. Knowledge of radiologic equipment and testing, physics, and radiation biology.

3. Knowledge of safety hazards of radiology and practice standards.

Skills:

1. Skill in basic and advanced positioning, including working with patients with implants.

2. Skill in applying compression.

3. Skill in providing adequate radiation protection.

Abilities:

1. Ability to pay attention to detail and to identify problems.

2. Ability to demonstrate genuine interest in working with people and to communicate clearly.

3. Ability to demonstrate full range of motion, finger/manual dexterity, and agility.

Equipment Operated: Standard and advanced mammography equipment.

Work Environment: Medical offices and mammography exam rooms. Exposure to radiation and communicable diseases. Must have 20/20 correctable vision.

Mental/Physical Requirements: Must be able to lift/carry/move items weighing up to 50 pounds. Requires positioning patients. Some stress related to anxious patients.

Nuclear Medicine Technologist

Job Title: Nuclear Medicine Technologist

Department: Radiology

Immediate Supervisor Title: Radiology Manager

Job Supervisory Responsibilities: May help supervise radiology technician

General Summary: A nonexempt position responsible for administering radiopharmaceuticals to patients for diagnostic purposes. May also perform radioimmunoassay studies.

Essential Job Responsibilities:

1. Explains test procedures to patients and prepares dosages of radio-pharmaceuticals.

2. Administers radiopharmaceuticals to patients by mouth, injection, inhalation, or other means. Positions patients on table or special chair. Adheres to safety standards that keep the radiation dose to patients and workers as low as possible.

3. Starts a gamma scintillation camera, or scanner, which creates images of the distribution of a radiopharmaceutical as it localizes in, and emits signals from, the patient's body. Operates the camera to detect and map the radioactive drug in the patient's body to create diagnostic images.

4. Monitors the characteristics and functions of tissues or organs in which the drugs localize to determine the presence of disease on the basis of biological changes rather than changes in organ structure.

5. Produces the images on a computer screen or on film for a physician to interpret.

6. Keeps patient records and records the amount and type of radionuclides received, used, and discarded.

7. Performs radioimmunoassay computerized studies as requested that assess the behavior of a radioactive substance inside the body to determine levels of hormones or of therapeutic drugs in the body.

Education: High school diploma. Successful completion of nuclear medicine technology program leading to an associate's or bachelor's degree.

Experience: Minimum two years of experience as nuclear medicine technician, preferably in medical practice setting.

Other Requirements: Most states require certification or licensure. Certification is available from the American Registry of Radiologic Technologists and from the Nuclear Medicine Technology Certification Board.

Performance Requirements: *Knowledge:*

1. Knowledge of the physical sciences, biological effects of radiation exposure, radiation protection and procedures.

2. Knowledge of radiopharmaceuticals, imaging techniques, and computer applications.

3. Knowledge of safety, infection control, quality assurance, and confidentiality regulations.

Skills:

1. Skill in sensitively understanding patients' physical and psychological needs.

2. Skill in paying attention to details and in following instructions.

3. Skill in administering radiopharmaceuticals and in operating camera and computer for imaging.

Abilities:

1. Ability to explain the procedure to patients in calm, accurate manner.

2. Ability to position patient and operate equipment effectively using mechanical abilities and manual dexterity.

3. Ability to interact effectively with physicians and other clinicians as a team member.

Equipment Operated: Imaging equipment including cameras and computers. Special tables/chairs for positioning patients. Safety equipment including shielded syringes, gloves, and other protective devices. Technologists wear badges that measure radiation levels.

Work Environment: Potential for radiation exposure is minimal because of safety precautions. Some exposure to communicable diseases and other conditions related to medical environment.

Mental/Physical Requirements: Physical stamina needed because technologists are on their feet much of the day and may lift or turn disabled patients. May be required to lift/turn up to 100+ pounds. Stress related to dealing with anxious patients and need to be accurate and safe.

Radiation Therapist

Job Title:	Radiation Therapist
Department:	Radiology Department, Laboratory Department, or Oncology Department
Immediate Supervisor Title:	Radiology Manager, Laboratory Manager, or Oncology Manager
Job Supervisory Responsibilities:	None
General Summary:	A nonexempt position responsible for administering radiation treatment to patients under the direction of a radiation oncologist.

Essential Job Responsibilities:

1. Prepares exam room and equipment. Explains procedure to patient. Takes medical history information if needed.

2. Uses an X-ray imaging machine to pinpoint the location of the tumor and/or computerized tomography (CT) scan to help determine how best to direct the radiation to minimize damage to healthy tissue. Positions patient and adjusts the linear accelerator to concentrate radiation exposure on the tumor cells following the treatment plan developed in conjunction with radiation oncologist. Explains procedure to the patient. Performs dosimetry procedures.

3. Delivers accurately the prescribed planned course of radiation therapy. Monitors patient's physical condition during treatment phase to determine any adverse side effects. Documents all pertinent information in medical record including dose of radiation used for each treatment, total amount of radiation used to date, area treated, and patient's reactions.

4. Performs daily linear accelerator warm-up procedures. Checks photon beam and all electron beams for consistency. Checks physics components for accuracy of beam alignment.

5. Cares for brachytherapy sources including preparing for use, cleaning and returning to safe, keeping log of use.

6. Follows radiation safety protocols in competent manner.

Education: Successful completion of an associate's or bachelor's degree program in radiation therapy or a radiography program, plus a 12-month certificate program in radiation therapy.

Experience: Minimum two years of experience as staff radiation therapist in radiation center, preferably in clinic setting.

Other Requirements: Some states require state license. Also required by some states and employers is certification by the American Registry of Radiologic Technologists.

Performance Requirements: *Knowledge:*

    1. Knowledge of radiation therapy theory and applications.

    2. Knowledge of radiation safety protocols.

    3. Knowledge of dosimetry and treatment planning.

Skills:

    1. Skill in effectively performing radiation procedures, particularly safety procedures.

    2. Skill in explaining radiation plans and treatments to patients and their families.

    3. Skill in identifying unsatisfactory set-up situations and/or errors and reporting them to radiation oncologist.

Abilities:

    1. Ability to observe and deal competently and compassionately with patient's emotional condition, maintaining a positive attitude and providing emotional support.

    2. Ability to collaborate effectively with health care team.

    3. Ability to demonstrate manual/finger dexterity, eye–hand coordination, and agility for use with equipment.

Equipment Operated: Radiation equipment and related items such as treatment table. Computer hardware and software for documentation purposes.

Work Environment: Medical offices and exam rooms. Clean, well lighted, and well ventilated. Exposure to radioactive materials and communicable diseases.

Mental/Physical Requirements: Considerable standing (four to six hours per day), walking, sitting, and stooping. May need to help transfer patients and lift/carry equipment weighing 75+ pounds. Stress related to need for safety and accuracy and dealing with anxious patients.

Sonographer/Ultrasonographer

Job Title:	Sonographer/Ultrasonographer
Department:	Laboratory, Obstetrics/Gynecology, or Clinical Services
Immediate Supervisor Title:	Laboratory, Obstetrics/Perinatologist, or Clinical Services Manager
Job Supervisory Responsibilities:	None

General Summary: A nonexempt position responsible for using diagnostic medical equipment to diagnose various medical conditions. Sonography, or ultrasonography, is the use of sound waves to generate an image for assessment and diagnosis. May specialize in obstetric/gynecologic, abdominal, neurosonograpy, or breast sonography.

Essential Job Responsibilities:

1. Reviews patient's medical history and physician's instructions. Prepares equipment for procedure. Selects appropriate equipment settings. Explains procedure to patient and records any medical history that may be relevant to the condition being viewed. Directs the patient to move into positions that will provide the best view.

2. Spreads gel on the skin to aid the transmission of sound waves.

3. Operates special equipment to direct nonionizing, high-frequency sound waves into areas of the patient's body. The equipment collects reflected echoes and forms an image that may be videotaped, transmitted, or photographed for interpretation and diagnosis by a physician.

4. Views the screen during the scan, looking for visual cues that contrast healthy areas with unhealthy ones. Selects images to show to the physician for diagnostic purposes. Takes measurements, calculates values, and analyzes the results in preliminary reports for the physicians.

5. Keeps patient records and adjusts/maintains equipment.

6. Complies with safety, infection control, and quality improvement policies/procedures.

Education: High school diploma. Associate's or bachelor's degree in sonography from accredited school. Training may be available in hospitals, vocational-technical institutions, and the Armed Forces.

Experience: Minimum one or more years of experience and/or training with graduate sonographer.

Other Requirements: No state license required. Certification of competency and registration available through organizations such as the American Registry for Diagnostic Medical Sonography. Registration requires passing a general physical principles and instrumentation examination, in addition to passing an exam in a specialty such as ob/gyn sonography, abdominal sonography, or neurosonography.

Performance Requirements: *Knowledge:*

1. Knowledge of anatomy, physiology, instrumentation, basic physics, patient care, and medical ethics.
2. Knowledge of mathematics and science.
3. Knowledge of safety, infection control, and quality improvement practices.

Skills:

1. Skill in communication and interpersonal interactions.
2. Skill in performing mathematical and scientific calculations.
3. Skill in gathering and analyzing patient data.

Abilities:

1. Ability to explain technical procedures and results to patients in user-friendly manner.
2. Ability to calm patients who may be nervous about the procedure.
3. Ability to use correct body mechanics to assist patients appropriately.

Equipment Operated: Variety of sonography equipment including ultrasound machines, transducers, gels, and computer hardware/software.

Work Environment: Combination of exam and laboratory rooms and darkroom. In some situations, may work in operating room. Sometimes works in close quarters. Exposure to communicable diseases, biohazards, and other conditions related to clinic settings.

Mental/Physical Requirements: May be standing for long periods and may have to lift/turn disabled patients. Work primarily at diagnostic imaging machines involving standing, sitting, walking, bending, lifting, and reaching. Some stress related to dealing with anxious patients.

X-Ray Technician

Job Title: X-Ray Technician

Department: X-Ray

Immediate Supervisor Title: Radiology Manager

Job Supervisory Responsibilities: None

General Summary: A nonexempt position responsible for operating X-ray and fluoroscopic equipment that assists radiologists and/or physicians with diagnosing and/or treating disease and/or injury.

Essential Job Responsibilities:
1. Prepares patients for radiologic procedures. Protects patient, self, and other staff from radiation hazards. Takes X-rays following established procedures for patient care and safety, which involves setting up and operating radiographic equipment used in the medical diagnosis and/or treatment of patients and includes implementing infection control procedures for the work area. Selects proper ionizing factors for radiological diagnosis. Adjusts/sets radiographic controls. Positions patients and takes X-rays of specific parts of the patient's body as requested by physicians. Processes film. Checks X-rays for clarity of image, retaking when needed. Distributes X-rays to appropriate medical staff.
2. Maintains required records including patient records, daily log books, and monthly reports. Performs quantity and quality control checks to assure X-ray unit meets standards required by laws, rules, and departmental policies. Complies with safety standards.
3. Cleans, maintains, and makes minor adjustments to radiographic equipment, including determining equipment repairs.
4. Maintains radiographic supplies, film, and orders as necessary.

Education: Associate's degree in radiological technology from accredited X-ray technician program.

Experience: One to three years of experience as X-ray technician, preferably in medical practice environment.

Other Requirements: American Registry of Radiologic Technologists registration preferred.

Performance Requirements: *Knowledge:*

1. Knowledge of X-ray procedures and protocols.

2. Knowledge of anatomy and physiology necessary to perform X-ray testing including body mechanics and patient movement.

3. Knowledge of radiology equipment including safety hazards common to radiology.

Skills:

1. Skill in positioning patients properly.

2. Skill in identifying equipment problems and correcting or notifying supervisor.

3. Skill in following infection control and radiological safety procedures.

Abilities:

1. Ability to lift and position patients for the type of X-ray procedure required.

2. Ability to notice detail in drawings and differences in shapes and shadings.

3. Ability to apply written instructions and standardized work practices.

Equipment Operated: Radiological equipment used for medical diagnosis and treatment.

Work Environment: Radiological unit. Exposure to disease, radiation, and toxic chemicals in the course of performing the work.

Mental/Physical Requirements: Standing six to eight hours per day, walking, stooping, and bending. Requires ability to move equipment and transfer patients. Occasional stress when working with anxious patients.

NURSING

- Certified Nursing Assistant/Nurse Aide
- Clinical Specialist
- Dialysis Nurse/Nephrology Nurse
- Director of Nursing
- Licensed Practice Nurse
- Medical Manager/Clinical Services Manager
- Nurse Manager
- Nurse Practitioner
- Oncology Nurse
- Registered Nurse
- Team Leader
- Telemonitoring Nurse
- Triage Telephone Nurse

Certified Nursing Assistant/Nurse Aide

Job Title: Certified Nursing Assistant/Nurse Aide

Department: Nursing

Immediate Supervisor Title: Nurse Manager. Also receives some supervision from RNs, LPNs, and physicians.

Job Supervisory Responsibilities: None

General Summary: A nonexempt position responsible for assisting nursing staff with basic care and for helping patients with activities of daily living under the supervision of an RN or LPN.

Essential Job Responsibilities:
1. Helps RN to gather medical history information. Provides routine patient care as outlined by state Nurse Practice Act, including following care plans, nursing assessments, administering medications, taking vital signs, and changing dressings.
2. Assists patients with activities of daily living including ambulation, transfers, dressing, grooming, and nutrition. Transports patients safely using appropriate equipment such as wheelchairs.
3. Observes patient condition and immediately communicates changes/concerns to RN or nurse manager. Documents patient information for medical record including vital signs and weight.
4. Follows emergency procedures including using CPR if necessary.
5. Helps stock department equipment and supplies.
6. Other duties as assigned.

Education: High school diploma preferred. Successful completion of state-approved certified nursing assistant training program; minimum 75 hours of training including 16 hours of supervised clinical training.

Experience: Minimum two years of experience as a certified nursing assistant. Minimum of one year clinic experience.

Other Requirements: Certification by state. Ongoing CPR certification.

Performance Requirements: *Knowledge:*

1. Knowledge of basic nursing skills with emphasis on activities of daily living.
2. Knowledge of ways to help RNs, LPNs, and physicians in clinic setting and to maintain a safe working environment.
3. Knowledge of body mechanics.

Skills:

1. Skill in appropriately taking vital signs and weights.
2. Skill in effectively transferring and transporting patients.
3. Skill in maintaining a clutter-free, organized exam area.

Abilities:

1. Ability to respond flexibly to changing workload or patient assignments.
2. Ability to use department supplies and equipment in a cost-efficient, effective manner.
3. Ability to communicate effectively as a health care team member.
4. Ability to demonstrate full range of motion, eye–hand coordination, manual/finger dexterity and agility.

Equipment Operated: Standard exam room and medical equipment, including wheelchairs.

Work Environment: Combination of office and exam rooms. Frequent exposure to communicable diseases, biohazards, toxic substances, medicinal preparations, and other conditions common to a clinic environment.

Mental/Physical Requirements: Varied activities including standing, sitting, walking, bending, and lifting. Occasionally lifts and carries items weighing up to 50 pounds. Occasional stress related to patient load.

Clinical Specialist

Job Title: Clinical Specialist

Department: Clinical Services

Immediate Supervisor Title: Director of Nursing or Clinical Services Manager

Job Supervisory Responsibilities: None

General Summary: An exempt position responsible for educating clinical and administrative staff about variety of topics ranging from new drugs, techniques/protocols, health-related governmental regulations, and legal matters. This professional position is often held by an advanced practice nurse or specialty expert who serves as a consultant/resource for the medical practice to support quality care.

Essential Job Responsibilities:

1. Serves as an educator, consultant, practitioner, and researcher to address a range of topics for clinicians and administrators. Provides expertise about clinical/health matters.

2. Participates in needs assessment, policy development, and program planning/implementation, providing leadership at senior level. Designs program guidelines, activities, and procedures to promote quality patient care.

3. Consults on complex patient medical issues relating to field of expertise and state-of-the-art clinical care.

4. Collects, analyzes, interprets data and presents information in formats that clarify the significance of the data to a variety of audiences. Prepares and disseminates information to illustrate ethical, political, scientific, economic, and other factors impacting the medical practice.

5. Plans/implements training and provides technical assistance to health providers in clinic and in community.

Education: Bachelor's degree in nursing (or other clinical specialty) and master's degree in nursing, community health, or other clinical specialty.

Experience: Extensive experience (5 to 10 years) in a relevant specialty clinical area, with at least 2 to 5 years in medical practice setting.

Other Requirements: Current state license in nursing or other specialty as necessary. Current CPR certificate.

Performance Requirements: *Knowledge:*

1. Knowledge of defined area of advanced practice in nursing and allied health services. Familiarity with state-of-the-art developments in medical field.

2. Knowledge of federal and state laws relating to nursing/clinical care, professional ethics related to the delivery of nursing/clinical care.

3. Knowledge of risk assessment, health status indicators, multicultural factors, and community health issues.

Skills:

1. Skill in collaborating with colleagues, providers, and patients to assess health needs of specific populations, developing strategies and specific programs to address these issues, and making presentations.

2. Skill in diagnosing and treating complex clinical cases as consultant to other providers.

3. Skill in staying on top of trends in medical field serving as proficient role model.

Abilities:

1. Ability to analyze complex data and draw conclusions needed to develop clinic policy and procedures.

2. Ability to communicate effectively with variety of internal and external groups.

3. Ability to facilitate discussion and build consensus.

Equipment Operated: Standard office equipment, particularly computer hardware and software programs for research and analysis. Clinical equipment and supplies as needed when providing patient care.

Work Environment: Primarily office setting with some activities in exam rooms. Some exposure to communicable diseases and conditions related to clinic setting.

Mental/Physical Requirements: Nonintense physical activity. Mostly sedentary. Some standing for presentations. Some stress related to handling complex cases and heavy workload.

Dialysis Nurse/Nephrology Nurse

Job Title: Dialysis Nurse/Nephrology Nurse

Department: Clinical Services or Dialysis Unit

Immediate Supervisor Title: Clinical Services Manager or Dialysis Unit Manager

Job Supervisory Responsibilities: May participate in supervising LPNs, CNAs, and medical assistants

General Summary: An exempt position responsible for providing care to patients who have kidney disease in a hemodialysis center.

Essential Job Responsibilities:

1. Checks on patients' vital signs and talks with them to assess their condition.
2. Teaches patients about their disease and its treatment and answers any questions.
3. Oversees the dialysis treatment from start to finish.
4. Makes sure patients are given the correct medications ordered by their physicians.
5. Evaluates patients' reactions to the dialysis treatment and medications.
6. Reviews the patients' lab work, home medications, and activities. Informs physicians about changes in their patients' conditions. Documents patient history and outcomes.
7. Other duties as assigned.

Education: RN required; BSN preferred with emphasis on nephrology and hemodialysis.

Experience: Minimum four to six years of experience as RN with at least two years in a dialysis unit.

Other Requirements: Current state RN license. Current CPR certificate. Desired for individual to be or become a certified nephrology nurse or certified dialysis nurse.

Performance Requirements: *Knowledge:*

1. Knowledge of nursing principles and procedures.

2. Knowledge of nephrology and dialysis.

3. Knowledge of quality assurance, infection control, safety, and confidentiality protocols and regulations.

Skills:

1. Skill in assessing patients' condition.

2. Skill in evaluating patients' learning needs and providing appropriate education about their treatment.

3. Skill in giving patients the medications ordered by their physicians.

Abilities:

1. Ability to analyze the patients' lab work, medications, and activities and confer with physicians on any changes.

2. Ability to evaluate the patients' capability to perform their dialysis treatments at home and take all prescribed medications.

3. Ability to work well in a team-focused environment.

Equipment Operated: Dialysis unit equipment, instruments, and supplies. Standard office equipment including computers for records and reports.

Work Environment: Medical office, exam rooms, and dialysis unit. Exposure to communicable diseases, biohazards, and other conditions related to medical setting.

Mental/Physical Requirements: Combination of standing, sitting, bending, walking, and reaching. Occasionally must lift/carry/move up to 50 pounds. Frequent stress related to dealing with patients suffering from kidney disease and coping with dialysis.

Director of Nursing

Job Title:	Director of Nursing
Department:	Clinical Services
Immediate Supervisor Title:	Clinical Services Manager or Senior Administrator
Job Supervisory Responsibilities:	RNs, LPNs, CNAs, and medical assistants
General Summary:	An exempt position responsible for all nursing staff and clinical nursing operations. May also have administrative responsibility for risk management, utilization management, reimbursement, and specific specialties such as critical care, cardiac care, women's health, or surgical units depending on the services offered by the medical practice.

Essential Job Responsibilities:

1. Participates at senior-management level in all planning, budgeting, policy making, and decision making related to clinical operations involving nursing staff.

2. Ensures that nursing aspects related to risk management, reimbursement, financial management, and other administrative functions are incorporated into operational systems. Monitors outcomes, budget results, patient satisfaction surveys, and other indicators of nursing performance.

3. Establishes a human resources plan for nursing including need for numbers and types of nurses and related allied health staff. Works with human resources specialist and nurse managers and team leaders to recruit, select, orient, and train new staff.

4. Makes sure the performance and productivity of all nursing staff are evaluated on a regular basis throughout the year and annually. Advises on appropriate corrective actions and development opportunities.

5. Maintains high quality of care by nursing staff through continuous improvement of standards and protocols. Ensures all staff are trained in quality assurance/control requirements and meet these standards.

6. Stays current with state, federal, and payer regulations/requirements and updates professional standards for nursing for the medical practice appropriately.

Education:	BSN required; MSN preferred or master's in business, health administration or other related field.
Experience:	Minimum 10 years of nursing experience with progressively increasing management/operations experience.
Other Requirements:	Current state RN license. Current CPR certification.

Performance Requirements:	*Knowledge:*

Knowledge:

1. Knowledge of nursing principles, practices, and procedures.
2. Knowledge of federal, state, and payer regulations and requirements related to nursing including patient safety, infection control, and confidentiality.
3. Knowledge of quality assurance, risk management, utilization management, and outcomes management standards.

Skills:

1. Skill in the human resource management of staff from recruitment through evaluation.
2. Skill in utilizing computerized systems to gather data, analyze results, and make recommendations.
3. Skill in developing/monitoring budgets and maintaining cost-effective nursing practices.

Abilities:

1. Ability to analyze data, problem solve, and make decisions related to nursing issues.
2. Ability to communicate with all levels and departments about nursing topics.
3. Ability to collaborate with senior managers to improve clinical operations.

Equipment Operated: Standard office equipment with emphasis on computer hardware and software. Occasional use of nursing equipment, particularly for training purposes.

Work Environment: Primarily medical offices. Rare contact with patients. Some external meetings with payers, regulators, and industry representatives.

Mental/Physical Requirements: Mostly sedentary. Some walking, standing, reaching, and bending. Rare need to lift/carry/move items weighing up to 25 pounds. High level of responsibility may create stress related to quality care and patient issues.

Licensed Practical Nurse

Job Title: Licensed Practical Nurse

Department: Clinical Services or Specialty Department

Immediate Supervisor Title: Director of Nursing, Nurse Manager, or Nursing Team Leader

Job Supervisory Responsibilities: None

General Summary: A nonexempt position responsible for nursing care under the supervision of physicians and clinical services manager.

Essential Job Responsibilities:

1. Obtains, verifies, and records health history of patients. Gathers pertinent health data through physical assessments and biological samples. Collects specimens for laboratory analysis.

2. Provides basic patient care as ordered. Administers medications and treatments as directed. Assists other health care professionals in performing exams, diagnostic procedures and treatments, and minor medical procedures. Adheres to infection control/safety guidelines and confidentiality policies.

3. Documents assessments, interventions, patient/family responses, medication dispensed/prescribed, and test results in medical records.

4. Promotes wellness by providing patient education materials, communicating physician advice/instructions.

Education: High school diploma. Graduation from an approved practical nursing program.

Experience: Minimum one year of LPN experience; clinic experience preferred.

Other Requirements: State-licensed practical nurse.

Performance Requirements: *Knowledge:*

1. Knowledge of medical terminology, anatomy, physiology, and pathophysiology. Familiarity with health care systems, regulations, policies, and functions. Understanding of documentation standards.

2. Knowledge of equipment, supplies, and materials needed for medical treatment. Understanding of basic laboratory procedures including preparation and screening.

3. Knowledge of infectious disease management and control and safety standards.

Skills:

1. Skill in reading and following written and oral medical orders.

2. Skill in initiating appropriate emergency procedures.

3. Skill in handling a number of tasks simultaneously.

4. Skill in performing blood draws.

Abilities:

1. Ability to use manual dexterity to perform medical treatments.

2. Ability to establish and maintain effective working relationships with coworkers and diverse patient populations.

3. Ability to perform mathematical calculations for drug dosages.

Equipment Operated: Phone, computer, medical charts, stethoscope, echocardiography (EKG) machine, ear-washing instruments, blood pressure cuff, speculums, and other nursing items. May involve use of walkers, wheelchairs, pulse oximetry, and oxygen tanks.

Work Environment: Medical exam and treatment rooms and medical offices. Environmental setting (lighting, temperature, air quality, acoustics) controlled.

Mental/Physical Requirements: Occasional exposure to communicable diseases and biohazards. Daily standing, squatting, walking, bending, and maneuvering. May require lifting up to 50 pounds to transfer/turn patient with/without assistive devices. Stress can be triggered by workload and difficult patients.

Medical Manager/Clinical Services Manager

Job Title: Medical Manager/Clinical Services Manager

Department: Applicable to multiple departments

Immediate Supervisor Title: Chief Executive Officer or Administrator

Job Supervisory Responsibilities: May supervise variety of staff including team leaders

General Summary: An exempt position responsible for planning, directing, coordinating, and supervising the delivery of health care. Must be prepared to deal with evolving integrated health care delivery systems, technological innovations, an increasingly complex regulatory environment, restructuring of work, and more emphasis on preventive care.

Essential Job Responsibilities:
1. Manages clinical department with major focus on improving the business aspects of health care operations and the quality of the health care provided.
2. Collaborates with administrative staff and physicians to optimize efficiency of a variety of related services ranging from inpatient care to outpatient follow-up care.
3. Establishes and implements policies, objectives, and procedures for department. Reports on department results and outcomes.
4. Participates in staff human resource planning and decisions, including hiring, training, supervision, and evaluating personnel and their work.
5. Develops budgets including recommendations for equipment outlays. Ensures appropriate reimbursement by staying abreast of billing, collections, and payer matters as well as Medicare/Medicaid regulations.
6. Coordinates activities with other clinical managers, administrative staff, and physicians.
7. Other duties as assigned.

Education: BSN or other clinical degree. Master's degree in health administration or business administration preferred. On-the-job management experience may be an acceptable substitute.

Experience: Minimum 5 to 10 years of clinical experience with business/management responsibilities.

Other Requirements: Current state RN license or other clinical license as required by state. Current CPR certification.

Performance Requirements:	*Knowledge:*

Knowledge:

1. Knowledge of payment/reimbursement systems and government/legal regulations and requirements related to health care.
2. Knowledge of health care delivery trends and implications for clinical specialty and for the medical practice.
3. Knowledge of planning, budgeting, human resource management, and report development. Understanding of cost analysis techniques.

Skills:

1. Skill in motivating others to implement their decisions, which requires strong leadership abilities using tact, diplomacy, flexibility, and communication techniques.
2. Skill in using financial and information systems.
3. Skill in restructuring work to make patient flow and other operational systems more efficient.

Abilities:

1. Ability to make effective decisions by being open to different opinions.
2. Ability to analyze contradictory information and solve problems effectively.
3. Ability to analyze financial and other business data.

Equipment Operated: Standard office equipment with emphasis on computer hardware and software.

Work Environment: Typically work in comfortable, private offices. Rare contact with patients.

Mental/Physical Requirements: Mostly a sedentary job. Considerable walking to consult with coworkers and staff. High level of stress related to multiple clinical and administrative responsibilities.

Nurse Manager

Job Title:	Nurse Manager
Department:	Clinical Services
Immediate Supervisor Title:	Director of Nurses or Clinical Services Manager
Job Supervisory Responsibilities:	Nursing staff and related medical support staff including RNs, LPNs, CNAs, and medical assistants
General Summary:	An exempt position responsible for managing the daily operations related to nursing care in line with clinical practice standards.

Essential Job Responsibilities:

1. Oversees clinical nursing care, ensuring compliance with established regulations and standards including quality assurance, confidentiality, and medical record documentation.

2. Provides direct supervision to nurses and subordinate staff, ensuring appropriate assessment and treatment of patient health. Serves as key problem-solving resource for staff on patient issues. Studies patient needs/trends and suggests solutions to ongoing patient care problems.

3. Collaborates with director of nurses/clinical services manager on development and implementation of nursing department's mission, goals, policies, procedures, budget quality assurance plan, and work standards.

4. Compiles/analyzes data on patient outcomes, quality assurance results, budget/goal achievement, and performance/productivity and prepares reports for administration.

5. Participates in medical practice planning related to clinic and emergency/disaster response system.

6. Analyzes staffing patterns with human resource specialist. Collaborates with human resources department on recruiting, selecting, orienting/training, and evaluating nursing staff.

Education:	BSN from accredited school of nursing. MSN preferred.
Experience:	Minimum five years of professional nursing experience including two years supervisory-level experience, preferably in medical practice setting.
Other Requirements:	Current state RN license. Current CPR certificate.

Performance Requirements: *Knowledge:*

1. Knowledge of nursing practice principles and techniques, occupational health and safety hazards and standards, and health care laws and regulations.

2. Knowledge of budgetary, supervisory, human resources, and quality-improvement principles and techniques.

3. Knowledge of clinical state-of-the-art advancements and trends in health care.

4. Knowledge of principles of employee development to ensure appropriate training and mentoring of staff.

Skills:

1. Skill in applying and modifying, as appropriate, the principles, methods, and techniques of professional nursing.

2. Skill in identifying problems, researching, and recommending solutions.

3. Skill in developing and maintaining high level of quality care/quality assurance.

4. Skill in exercising high degree of initiative, judgment, discretion, and decision making.

Abilities:

1. Ability to manage the overall provision of nursing services and build consensus among staff.

2. Ability to work effectively with diverse individuals at all levels of the medical practice.

3. Ability to handle many tasks simultaneously and deal effectively with changing priorities.

4. Ability to demonstrate full range of motion including handling and lifting patients, manual and finger dexterity, and eye–hand coordination.

Equipment Operated: Standard nursing equipment and office equipment including computer hardware and software.

Work Environment: Combination of office, exam, and other clinical settings. Frequent exposure to communicable diseases, biohazards, toxic substances, medicinal preparations, and other conditions common to a clinic setting.

Mental/Physical Requirements: Requires standing and walking for extensive periods of time. Occasionally lifts and carries items weighing up to 50 pounds. Occasional stress caused by multitasking and level of responsibility.

Nurse Practitioner

Job Title:	Nurse Practitioner
Department:	Nursing
Immediate Supervisor Title:	Clinical Services Manager or Director of Nursing
Job Supervisory Responsibilities:	May share in the supervision of RNs, LPNs, and/or medical assistants, depending on departmental organization
General Summary:	An exempt position responsible for providing primary care services, including assessing, diagnosing, prescribing, treating, and educating patients. Works closely with physicians and other clinicians in a team approach to patient care. May specialize in a specific type of clinical care, e.g., pediatrics, geriatrics.

Essential Job Responsibilities:

1. Assesses patient status by obtaining health history through patient/family interviews and chart reviews; assessing presenting illness, risk factors, and family history, psychosocial situation, and cultural factors; and performing appropriate physical examination.

2. Orders/performs appropriate laboratory diagnostic and other screening tests. Seeks other information as needed, including consultation with physicians and other clinicians, for evaluation of illness. Integrates data to determine diagnosis and therapeutic plan, including identification of any health risks.

3. Develops and implements treatment plan by prescribing/dispensing medications and/or injections in compliance with medical practice guidelines and state laws. Handles minor lacerations. Instructs patient/family regarding medications and treatments. Educates patients regarding health promotion/illness prevention. Recommends appropriate community resources to meet patient/family needs. Communicates appropriate case management information to other professionals and community agencies. Prepares documentation for medical records including updating patient medical chart by posting examination and test results, diagnosis, medications, and treatment in written/computerized manner.

4. Participates in peer reviews, chart reviews, staff education, clinical guideline development, and other continuing education and quality assurance activities to demonstrate compliance with standards, regulations, policies, and procedures. Acts as consultant/collaborator to clinical team on area of specialty. Complies with patient confidentiality requirements. Promotes patient advocacy.

5. Collaborates with physicians in managing acute and long-term medical needs of patient. Provides monitoring and continuity of care between visits according to treatment plan including triaging patient calls/e-mails.

Education:	BSN required; MSN preferred. Successful completion of advanced practitioner training and certification as a practitioner (general or specialized) from an approved nurse practitioner program.
Experience:	Minimum three years of professional nursing experience in a clinic setting, plus two years of nurse practitioner experience.
Other Requirements:	Current state registered nurse license. Current state license as an advanced registered nurse practitioner with prescriptive authority. Current CPR certification.

Performance Requirements: *Knowledge:*

1. Knowledge of advanced practice of nursing including anatomy and physiology, pathophysiology, pharmacology and therapeutics, basic nutrition, behavioral factors, psychosocial/family systems, diagnostic testing, interpretation of results and clinical decision making, alternative treatment modalities.

2. Knowledge of professional nursing theory, practices and regulations related to evaluating and providing patient care, and professional ethics related to the delivery of nursing care.

3. Knowledge of medical equipment and instruments used to administer patient care.

4. Knowledge of common safety hazards and precautions to establish/ maintain a safe work environment.

5. Knowledge of health promotion, health risk identification, and patient education principles and techniques.

6. Knowledge of community, professional, and educational resources.

Skills:

1. Skill in oral and written communication including interviewing to gather medical histories; providing presentations, consultations, facilitation, and documentation, e.g., writing medical orders, patient education materials, and medical record updates. May require skill in using computerized health information management systems.

2. Skill in case management, time management, problem solving, crisis intervention, multitasking, and other organizational matters.

3. Skill in modifying methods and techniques of professional nursing to provide appropriate nursing care and in initiating appropriate emergency response and investigatory procedures.

Abilities:

1. Ability to analyze complex data and draw conclusions.

2. Ability to interpret, adapt, and apply guidelines and procedures.

3. Ability to establish/maintain effective working relationships with patients, clinical staff, and the public.

Equipment Operated: Standard medical examination room equipment and instruments. May include use of computer/health information management system.

Work Environment: Combination of exam rooms and medical offices. Frequent exposure to communicable diseases, toxic substances, ionizing radiation, medicinal preparations, and other conditions common to a clinic environment.

Mental/Physical Requirements: Requires standing and walking for extensive periods of time. Occasionally requires lifting and carrying items weighing up to 10 pounds. Requires correct vision and hearing to normal range. Requires working under stress in emergency situations and occasionally may involve irregular working hours.

Oncology Nurse

Job Title:	Oncology Nurse
Department:	Oncology or Clinical Services
Immediate Supervisor Title:	Oncology Manager or Clinical Services Manager
Job Supervisory Responsibilities:	May supervise LPNs, CNAs, or medical assistants
General Summary:	An exempt position responsible for providing nursing care to individuals with cancer, at risk for developing cancer, or surviving cancer.

Essential Job Responsibilities:

1. Functions as a coordinator of care, collaborating with other cancer care providers and team members to provide required care as effectively as possible at all stages of illness from diagnosis to terminal.
2. Provides health care, education, and counseling for cancer prevention, screening, and detection.
3. Works with the multidisciplinary oncology team to achieve realistic health care goals for an individual diagnosed with cancer.
4. Participates in providing treatment specific to type of cancer, which may include chemotherapy, radiation, bone marrow transplant, or palliative care. Documents patient information and treatment steps/results.
5. Manages illness- and treatment-related symptoms. Helps patients live with cancer, retaining autonomy and independence. Utilizes most appropriate pain management techniques.
6. Utilizes an empathic and caring approach to patients whose diagnosis and treatment are often painful and life-threatening.

Education:	RN/BSN with a cancer-specific knowledge base and demonstrated clinical expertise in cancer care beyond that acquired in a basic nursing program. Advanced oncology nursing practice requires a minimum of a master's degree.
Experience:	Minimum four to six years of RN experience with oncology emphasis.
Other Requirements:	Current state RN license. Current CPR certificate. Preferred: Becoming an oncology certified nurse, advanced oncology certified nurse, or a certified pediatric oncology nurse.

Performance Requirements: *Knowledge:*

1. Knowledge of nursing principles and practices.

2. Knowledge of oncology practices and treatments.

3. Knowledge of state-of-the-art developments in cancer diagnosis and therapy.

Skills:

1. Skill in providing expertise about oncology to colleagues, allied health personnel, and health care consumers as preventive health education.

2. Skill in designing and performing a variety of patient education activities.

3. Skill in administering chemotherapy and other treatment therapies.

Abilities:

1. Ability to empathize with patients and families and to deal with grief and difficult patient interactions.

2. Ability to collaborate with health care team to make individualized treatment plans for each cancer patient.

3. Ability to cope with death and dying.

Equipment Operated: Clinical equipment, instruments, and supplies appropriate for oncology unit. Standard office equipment for records and reports.

Work Environment: Medical exam rooms, offices, and treatment rooms. Exposure to communicable diseases and biohazards and other conditions related to medical setting.

Mental/Physical Requirements: Combination of standing, sitting, bending, and reaching. Occasional need to lift/carry/move items weighing up to 50 pounds. Stress related to interactions with patients dealing with life-threatening illness.

Registered Nurse

Job Title:	Registered Nurse
Department:	Clinical Services or Specialty Department
Immediate Supervisor Title:	Nurse Manager, Clinical Services Manager, or a physician
Job Supervisory Responsibilities:	May participate in supervision of medical assistants, medical administrative assistants, licensed practical nurses, and certified nursing assistants
General Summary:	An exempt position responsible for providing primary care to patients, including assessment, treatment, care planning, and medical care evaluation.

Essential Job Responsibilities:

1. Obtains patient consent for care and ensures patient confidentiality. Obtains and documents health history, information on chief complaint, vital signs, and health risk factors and assesses disease condition. Provides patient care based on practice guidelines, standards of care, and federal/state laws and regulations.

2. Executes prescribed treatments and medical interventions, administers prescribed medications, and monitors and documents treatment progress and patient response. Delegates as allowed under the Nurse Practice Act. Refers to/consults with physicians, other health providers, and community resources to prevent/resolve problems or concerns. Educates patients and families about health status, health maintenance, and management of acute and chronic conditions.

3. Documents patient assessment and intervention data using established medical record forms/automated systems and documentation practices.

4. Participates in multidisciplinary teams to improve patient care processes and outcomes. Tracks quality assurance data and monitors for acute and chronic care management.

Education:	RN. Completion of nursing training from an accredited school of nursing. BSN preferred.
Experience:	Minimum one year of professional nursing experience. Clinic experience preferred.
Other Requirements:	Current state registered nurse license. Current CPR certificate.

Performance Requirements: *Knowledge:*

1. Knowledge of nursing processes; health care systems, structure, and functions; and community resources. Understanding of health care technology, equipment, and supplies. Familiarity with state law on nursing care, nurse practice guidelines, and clinic policies and procedures.

2. Knowledge of wellness/illness, growth and development, human behavior, psychosocial factors, and alternative health care treatments.

3. Knowledge of chart/medical record documentation requirements and federal/state laws related to release of health care information.

Skills:

1. Skill in time management, problem solving, multitasking, prioritizing, and medical care coordination.

2. Skill in initiating appropriate crisis interventions and emergency response.

3. Skill in patient triage in person and on the phone.

Abilities:

1. Ability to analyze options and then counsel patients and families about choices and make referrals to other providers and resources.

2. Ability to engage clients and families in the development and implementation of a care plan.

3. Ability to read and interpret physicians' orders and notes from other providers.

4. Ability to calculate and administer drug dosages and injections and measure results.

Equipment Operated: Standard nursing equipment and supplies including thermometer and syringes. May involve use of assistive devices such as walkers, wheelchairs, ventilators, pulse oximetry units, and oxygen tanks. May require use of computer.

Work Environment: Medical exam/treatment rooms and medical offices. Controlled lighting, acoustics, air quality, and temperature settings. Environmental hazards may be unpredictable including exposure to communicable diseases and biohazards.

Mental/Physical Requirements: Involves standing, walking, bending, grasping, manipulating, and squatting. Occasional need to lift patient during transfer/turn process with or without assistance. Stress can be triggered by workload and complex cases.

Team Leader

Job Title:	Team Leader
Department:	Applicable to Nursing and other clinical departments
Immediate Supervisor Title:	Department Manager
Job Supervisory Responsibilities:	May participate in supervision of line clinicians, including RNs, LPNs, CNAs, therapists, medical assistants, and medical administrative assistants
General Summary:	An exempt position responsible for day-to-day supervision of nurses or other clinicians and allied health staff within specific clinical protocols.

Essential Job Responsibilities:

1. Participates in the hiring, supervision, and evaluation of assigned staff.
2. Schedules staffing to meet changing workload needs.
3. Provides professional and technical support to staff and troubleshoots the delivery of patient care. Responds to requests from ombudsman, families, and other concerned patients regarding patient care issues.
4. Identifies training needs for staff and facilitates staff development. Participates in the development, implementation, and evaluation of training, orientation, and education programs.
5. Develops, implements, monitors, and evaluates quality assurance activities, ensuring compliance with standards, laws, regulations, and procedures. Recommends new and/or revised policies and procedures to the department manager.
6. Reviews and uses clinical and medical records to determine health care patterns and assignment of appropriate resources. Ensures corrective actions.

Education:	Bachelor's degree in clinical field, e.g., BSN.
Experience:	Minimum five years of experience in increasingly responsible clinical positions including some experience with supervision of clinicians.
Other Requirements:	Current RN or other clinical license as required. Current CPR certificate.

Performance Requirements: *Knowledge:*

1. Knowledge of clinical and theoretical nursing/clinical processes and principles. Familiar with state and federal laws related to health care.

2. Knowledge of human resources management principles.

3. Knowledge of medical practice protocols and standards.

Skills:

1. Skill in applying quality assurance techniques.

2. Skill in training staff, both new staff members and existing ones.

3. Skill in documentation of patient care including reviewing for accuracy and completeness.

Abilities:

1. Ability to communicate clearly with many different levels of staff.

2. Ability to analyze medical records and documentation and identify problem areas.

3. Ability to collaborate effectively with nursing and other clinical managers, physicians, and administrative staff.

Equipment Operated: Standard clinical and office equipment.

Work Environment: Combination of medical office and exam rooms. Frequent exposure to communicable diseases, biohazards, and other conditions common in clinic settings.

Mental/Physical Requirements: Variety of walking, standing, sitting, bending, twisting, and reaching. Occasional need to lift/carry/move up to 50 pounds of equipment. Frequent stress if dealing with multiple tasks and staff.

Telemonitoring Nurse

Job Title:	Telemonitoring Nurse
Department:	Clinical Services
Immediate Supervisor Title:	Clinical Services Manager
Job Supervisory Responsibilities:	None
General Summary:	An exempt position responsible for providing telemonitoring clinical services and support including assessment and patient education. May be outsourced to home health agency.

Essential Job Responsibilities:

1. Arranges for telemonitoring services, at direction of physician, for patient with chronic illness who needs ongoing monitoring of vital signs and compliance with physician orders.

2. Visits patient at home to discuss the service and get acceptance for the telemonitoring.

3. Installs equipment, which typically includes the clock-radio–sized monitor, and attachments such as a scale, blood pressure monitor, and pulse oximeter. May also include attachment to capture diabetic measurements. May also include video component so RN and/or physician can receive visuals of patient and facilitate two-way communication. Plugs into standard telephone line for transmission of data.

4. Explains procedure to patient and family including taking vital signs on schedule ordered by physician (at least three times per week) with the monitor and attachments and transmitting them to the telemonitoring RN at the medical practice/or contractor.

5. Analyzes vital-sign data on day received to ensure measurements are within parameters established by physician. Calls patient if significant variance to determine reason, e.g., patient deviated from diet or forgot to take medication. If reason cannot be determined or assessment seems to indicate an emergency, RN makes appropriate response ranging from arranging for an ambulance to sending patient to emergency room or setting up a visit with the physician.

6. Tracks patterns to ascertain any deviations over time. Compiles data into reports for physician on specified schedule, e.g., weekly, monthly, quarterly. Consults regularly with physician on patient status and outcomes of telemonitoring. Documents outcomes in patient record.

Education:	RN degree. BSN preferred. MSN helpful. On-the-job training or attendance at equipment contractor workshops to learn about instrumentation.
Experience:	Minimum five to seven years of experience as RN; minimum one to two years of experience as telemonitoring RN.
Other Requirements:	Current state RN license. Current CPR certificate. Must have valid driver's license or public transportation access to reach patients' homes.

Performance Requirements: *Knowledge:*

1. Knowledge of telemonitoring protocols related to monitoring chronic illness.
2. Knowledge of telemonitors and related equipment.
3. Knowledge of chronic care management.

Skills:

1. Skill in installing and maintaining telemonitoring equipment.
2. Skill in staying current with changes in telemonitoring technology.
3. Skill in responding quickly and calmly to emergencies.

Abilities:

1. Ability to educate patients about telemonitoring and to encourage them to comply with care plan defined by physician.
2. Ability to gather data, develop reports, analyze trends, and recommend any needed changes in plan of care.
3. Ability to collaborate effectively with physicians and other clinicians on best use of telemonitoring to improve quality of care.

Equipment Operated: Standard office equipment with emphasis on computer hardware and software analysis and reporting. Telemonitoring equipment.

Work Environment: Varied work settings including medical office, exam rooms, and patient homes. Exposure to communicable diseases and biohazards.

Mental/Physical Requirements: Combination of walking, sitting, standing, bending, reaching. Occasionally must lift/carry/move equipment weighing up to 50 pounds. Low level of stress unless patient emergency.

Triage Telephone Nurse

Job Title: Triage Telephone Nurse

Department: Clinical Services

Immediate Supervisor Title: Clinical Services Manager

Job Supervisory Responsibilities: None

General Summary: An exempt position responsible for providing triage (sorting/prioritizing patients) telephone service to ensure prompt identification of patients with high-risk conditions. May outsource this service to contractor.

Essential Job Responsibilities:

1. Talks directly to patients on the telephone and then directs them to emergency rooms (ERs) or urgent care centers or to see their physician during office hours.
2. Performs short evaluation of the patient situation to estimate severity of illness and/or injury including learning about chief complaint and, as possible, obtaining vital sign and mental status information.
3. Determines urgency of seeing the patient based on brief assessment and on familiarity with a patient's condition and history. May use computerized medical information database, which uses algorithms that closely imitate physician logic and thought patterns, as guide. Confers with physician as needed.
4. Sends those with high-risk chief complaints such as chest pain, abdominal pain, or severe headaches to ER immediately or arranges for ambulance. May provide appropriate home health advice to those patients who do not need to go directly to the ER.
5. Sets up appointment for patients who do not need to go to ER but need to see a physician or arranges for an appointment scheduler to make the appointment.
6. Acts, when designated, in "Ask a Nurse" capacity, handling routine information requests from patients, e.g., "Do I need a flu shot every year? When are you giving these shots?"

Education: RN degree; BSN or MSN degree preferred. On-the-job training in triage.

Experience: Minimum five years of experience as RN; one to two years of telephone triage experience, preferably in medical practice setting.

Other Requirements: Current state RN license. Current CPR certificate.

Performance Requirements: *Knowledge:*

1. Knowledge of telephone-based clinical assessment techniques.

2. Knowledge of medical practice telephone triage protocols.

3. Knowledge of appropriate home health information for patients to follow until visit with physician, if they do not need an immediate ER visit.

Skills:

1. Skill in using electronic medical records to check patient history.

2. Skill in using computerized medical information database during evaluation as guide to appropriate decision.

3. Skill in making triage decisions and responding quickly and calmly in emergency situations such as calling 911 and arranging for ambulance.

Abilities:

1. Ability to communicate clearly and calmly with patient.

2. Ability to elicit information needed to make brief evaluation.

3. Ability to work closely with physicians and other clinicians as needed.

Equipment Operated: Telephone system at medical practice or contractor office. Computer hardware/software for access to patient history and medical information databases.

Work Environment: Office setting, well lighted, good air quality. Rare direct contact with patients.

Mental/Physical Requirements: Mostly sedentary position. Hand/arm injury possible from repetitive movements. Stress generated if high volume of calls and emergencies.

PATIENT RELATIONS

- Health Educator
- Interpretive Services Coordinator
- Patient Representative/Advocate

Health Educator

Job Title: Health Educator

Department: Clinical Services or Community Health

Immediate Supervisor Title: Health Education Manager, Clinical Services Manager, or Community Health Manager

Job Supervisory Responsibilities: None

General Summary: An exempt position responsible for designing and providing patient and community health education with an emphasis on patient instruction related to a variety of topics including prevention and wellness initiatives.

Essential Job Responsibilities:

1. Designs and conducts educational programs and training for clinic staff and the community for patients, various public groups, and health care professionals based on analysis of patient and community needs.

2. Develops and promotes educational/informational materials and workshops that are accurate, culturally appropriate, and educationally sound.

3. Provides health education consultation for staff, patients, and the community on preventative health/health promotion needs and ways to address them. Collaborates with clinic departments and external resources to develop broad-based solutions to community health issues.

4. Coordinates community and medical practice partnerships including participating in public health fairs and events.

5. Participates in health policy development internally and externally as appropriate.

6. Other duties as assigned.

Education: Bachelor's degree in community health or nursing. Master's degree in education, curriculum development, or health education/instruction preferred.

Experience: Minimum two years of experience in health education, preferably in clinic setting.

Other Requirements: Some states or medical practices may require a continuing teaching certificate and/or a certified health education certificate.

Performance Requirements: *Knowledge:*

1. Knowledge of educational program planning, implementation, and evaluation.

2. Knowledge of training principles and methods, needs-assessment course design, and program evaluation. Understanding of research and analysis techniques.

3. Knowledge of patient education and community health theories and practices related to disease prevention, behavioral change, and methods of instruction.

Skills:

1. Skill in utilizing marketing principles and public information resources to promote programs.

2. Skill in consulting with patients and clinicians about health education topics.

3. Skill in use of computer hardware and software programs.

4. Skill in conducting training and making group presentations.

Abilities:

1. Ability to communicate effectively both orally and in writing.

2. Ability to communicate appropriately on interpersonal level with variety of audiences.

3. Ability to analyze patient information, community data, and program outcomes.

Equipment Operated: Standard office equipment and training equipment including wide range of audiovisual machines.

Work Environment: Mix of medical office and clinic exam rooms, as well as classroom clinics in the medical practice and in community centers.

Mental/Physical Requirements: May involve standing and sitting up to six to eight hours per day. Occasional lifting and carrying equipment up to 25 pounds. Usually low stress level.

Interpretive Services Coordinator

Job Title:	Interpretive Services Coordinator
Department:	Clinical Services
Immediate Supervisor Title:	Clinical Services Manager or Patient Services Manager
Job Supervisory Responsibilities:	Oversees contract interpreters/translators

General Summary: An exempt position responsible for ensuring that interpretation and translation services are available to patients and staff in line with federal mandate that health care providers ensure accurate communication in any language. May personally provide some of these services and may manage the outsourcing of other services to contractors.

Essential Job Responsibilities:

1. Translates written health care materials, health education materials, and administrative forms from English into specified language, e.g., Spanish, Vietnamese, Russian.

2. Performs oral interpretive services between medical staff and patients/families to facilitate communication in a variety of clinical settings to overcome any language and cultural barriers to understanding. Conducts phone interviews, coordinates appointments, and documents relevant information under the direction of the provider. May travel to satellite offices, contractor offices, and community outreach centers.

3. Interviews patients/families to gather information on medical histories and patient complaints/concerns/questions. Translates information into English-written medical records, documenting diagnosis, recommendations, and instructions. Records progress elicited in ongoing visits.

4. Assists providers in educating patients on diseases, disease prevention, clinic procedures, immunization schedules, and health management.

5. Identifies qualified contractors who can provide similar services in other languages. Maintains database of outsource services including those who can provide translation/interpretation in person or remotely by phone or other electronic means. Ensures both linguistic and medical terminology competence.

6. Other duties as assigned.

Education: High school diploma required; college degree with emphasis on language skills preferred. Course work in basic anatomy and medical terminology.

Experience: Minimum three years of experience as professional translator/interpreter, preferably in clinic setting.

Other Requirements: May require medical interpreter's certificate from state. Clinic may require successful completion of translation examples, interpreter practice sessions, and medical terminology tests.

Performance Requirements:	*Knowledge:*

Knowledge:

1. Knowledge of written translation techniques and principles.

2. Knowledge of linguistics in English and specified language(s). Understanding of ethical standards in language interpretation field.

3. Knowledge of specified culture's beliefs and values, particularly those related to health care. Familiar with community resources for specified target population, including refugee and immigrant social services.

4. Knowledge of human anatomy, clinical procedures/protocols, and medical terminology.

Skills:

1. Skill in identifying and managing competent translator/interpreter contractors.

2. Skill in using interview techniques.

3. Skill in identifying appropriate community resources.

Abilities:

1. Ability to communicate in culturally sensitive, confidential manner while interpreting.

2. Ability to collaborate closely with health care team to ensure clinicians obtain accurate information and patient/family are fully informed.

3. Ability to analyze psychosocial aspects of culture and problem solve appropriately.

Equipment Operated: Standard office equipment, including computer hardware and software.

Work Environment: Medical office and exam rooms. Some travel to satellite offices and community cultural centers. Occasional exposure to communicable diseases.

Mental/Physical Requirements: Mostly sedentary. Some standing, walking, and bending. Some stress related to ensuring accuracy of translation/interpretation and dealing with patients who may be confused about instructions.

Patient Representative/Advocate

Job Title: Patient Representative/Advocate

Department: Clinical Services

Immediate Supervisor Title: Clinical Services Manager

Job Supervisory Responsibilities: None

General Summary: A nonexempt position responsible for working directly with patients and their families to discuss any questions, complaints, comments, or suggestions. Advocates for patient in resolution of concerns.

Essential Job Responsibilities:
1. Serves as the clinic contact to resolve patient/family concerns and complaints.
2. Gathers and researches appropriate information related to patient care, reimbursement, or community resource issues. Follows complaint through to resolution and provides feedback to patient/family. Facilitates relationships with public.
3. Works with staff to resolve concerns and improve services, taking advocacy position.
4. Tracks and analyzes all concerns and complaints. Identifies problematic trends and makes recommendations for correction. Produces regular overview reports.
5. Develops referral systems with human services agencies and collaborates with community resource network.

Education: Bachelor's degree in human relations/social services, communications, marketing, or business/health administration.

Experience: Minimum two years of experience in customer services, with at least six months of experience in health care setting. Patient representative experience preferred.

Other Requirements: None

Performance Requirements: *Knowledge:*

1. Knowledge of health care field; medical practice clinical and administrative systems, departments, and practices, including clinic financial policies and reimbursement payment requirements.
2. Knowledge of counseling, conflict resolution, and customer service principles and applications.
3. Knowledge of research methods to identify issues and clarify policies. Understanding of medical terminology. Familiarity with community resources.

Skills:

1. Skill in analyzing data, policies, and requirements and in preparing objective, comprehensive reports using computers for both research and reporting.
2. Skill in defusing tense situations through diplomatic problem-solving.
3. Skill in effectively balancing needs of clinic with needs of patient with minimum of tension.

Abilities:

1. Ability to communicate effectively with patients, staff, and external contacts via phone, in person, and through well-written reports.
2. Ability to demonstrate leadership within medical practice to resolve immediate and long-term patient concerns.
3. Ability to establish/maintain effective relationships with a wide variety of people.

Equipment Operated: Standard office equipment with emphasis on computer hardware and software.

Work Environment: Primarily clinic office setting. Some travel within the community. Constant contact with individuals from many backgrounds. Minimum exposure to communicable diseases. Frequent stress from dealing with tense individuals in uncomfortable situations.

Mental/Physical Requirements: Combination of sitting, walking, and standing. May require sitting at computer workstation for one to two hours per day. Occasional stress from dealing with complex patient advocacy issues.

QUALITY IMPROVEMENT

- Quality Improvement Clinical Analyst
- Quality Improvement Coordinator
- Quality Improvement Manager

Quality Improvement Clinical Analyst

Job Title: Quality Improvement Clinical Analyst

Department: Quality Improvement

Immediate Supervisor Title: Quality Improvement Manager

Job Supervisory Responsibilities: None

General Summary: An exempt position responsible for supporting quality improvement (QI) efforts by conducting and coordinating clinical outcomes management efforts.

Essential Job Responsibilities:

1. Assists the QI manager in conducting a comprehensive, continuous quality improvement (CQI) program throughout the medical practice, including helping to develop annual plans and outcome goals and analyze results on an ongoing basis. Uses outcomes management computerized information systems to statistically analyze outcomes data including practice patterns.

2. Helps clinical teams to gather outcomes information following regulatory and accreditation standards. Compiles data into reports for the QI manager, and QI committee, and the senior management team, including an analysis of trends and patterns. Fulfills internal and external requests for outcomes data, including developing special reports.

3. Participates in presentations to educate staff on outcomes management principles and systems. Meets with clinical teams about outcomes data to discuss implications for clinical practices. Identifies areas needing improvement.

4. Collaborates with clinical teams to use outcomes data in patient education and clinical practice applications including the development of new condition-specific protocols and clinical documentation procedures. Helps train clinicians on new protocols.

Education: BSN or similar clinical degree. Master's degree in clinical field or health administration preferred.

Experience: Minimum three years of nursing or other clinical experience and two years of QI experience, preferably in medical practice setting.

Other Requirements: Current RN or other clinical license as required by state. Current CPR certificate.

Performance Requirements:	*Knowledge:*

Knowledge:

1. Knowledge of CQI and outcomes management principles and practices.
2. Knowledge of CQI software programs.
3. Knowledge of medical field and physician practice management.

Skills:

1. Skill in effective use of quality and outcomes management tools.
2. Skill in producing variety of outcomes reports.
3. Skill in appropriate implementation into clinical practices.

Abilities:

1. Ability to analyze outcomes data and use statistical methods to identify trends and patterns and make independent judgments.
2. Ability to make presentations and train staff in appropriate use of new clinical protocols aimed at improving outcomes.
3. Ability to interact effectively as member of health care team.

Equipment Operated: Standard office equipment with emphasis on computer hardware and software.

Work Environment: Office and classroom settings. Minimal contact with patients.

Mental/Physical Requirements: Primarily sitting, with some standing during classroom presentations. May need to lift/carry/move audiovisual training equipment weighing up to 50 pounds. Some stress related to need for accuracy.

Quality Improvement Coordinator

Job Title: Quality Improvement Coordinator

Department: Quality Improvement

Immediate Supervisor Title: Quality Improvement Manager

Job Supervisory Responsibilities: None

General Summary: An exempt position responsible for coordinating quality management efforts including development, implementation, education, data collection, and analysis.

Essential Job Responsibilities:

1. Helps quality improvement (QI) manager to plan, design, implement, and maintain a comprehensive medical practice continuous quality improvement (CQI) program including utilization management and risk management. Assists in educating new staff, including physicians, about QI systems and requirements.

2. Meets with internal and external audiences to identify and problem solve QI issues.

3. Monitors medical practice efforts to ensure compliance with internal and external QI standards. Reviews medical records and other documentation to ensure quality care. Helps to prepare annual QI report.

4. Coordinates the effort to gather data and prepare reports to meet the requirements of the National Committee for Quality Assurance (NCQA) and other regulatory/accrediting agencies, including patient satisfaction data.

5. Evaluates variance and other data to identify QI opportunities and risk management issues.

6. Monitors utilization and service quality through diagnosis-related group (DRG) review, Healthplan Employer Data and Information Set (HEDIS) quality measures, payer/provider/patient satisfaction surveys, and complaints. Follows through on complaints including identification of corrective actions needed. Reports on results.

Education: Bachelor's degree in health administration or health-related field. BSN preferred.

Experience: Minimum four years of experience in health care setting with minimum three years of experience in quality management, preferably in medical practice setting.

Other Requirements: Current RN state license. Current CPR certificate.

Performance Requirements: *Knowledge:*

1. Knowledge of CQI principles, practices, methods, and tools.
2. Knowledge of computer applications related to QI, including spreadsheets.
3. Knowledge of medical records and clinical care processes.

Skills:

1. Skill in effective education and facilitation of CQI efforts in medical practice.
2. Skill in application of analytical methods and statistical software by developing appropriate reports.
3. Skill in conducting QI checks of medical records and other clinical documentation and performing patient satisfaction surveys.

Abilities:

1. Ability to educate staff in both verbal and written form about QI in formal and informal settings.
2. Ability to interact effectively with health care team members.
3. Ability to analyze QI data and identify trends and corrective actions.

Equipment Operated: Standard office equipment including computer hardware and software.

Work Environment: Primarily office and classroom settings. Rare patient contact.

Mental/Physical Requirements: Combination of office and classroom settings. May occasionally need to lift/carry/move audiovisual equipment weighing up to 50 pounds. Occasional stress related to deadline pressure.

Quality Improvement Manager

Job Title:	Quality Improvement Manager
Department:	Quality Improvement
Immediate Supervisor Title:	Clinical Services Manager
Job Supervisory Responsibilities:	Quality Improvement Clinical Analyst and Clinical Outcomes Specialist
General Summary:	An exempt position responsible for identifying, implementing, monitoring, and evaluating clinical quality improvement (QI) activities and providing related consulting and support services.

Essential Job Responsibilities:

1. Participates in strategic and operational planning at senior level to ensure quality care. Integrates the principles and values of continuous quality improvement (CQI) throughout the medical practice. Ensures that CQI efforts comply with regulatory and accreditation standards. Meets requirements related to utilization management and risk management.

2. Collaborates with chief technology officer to ensure data systems and programs satisfactorily support CQI activities, including maintaining QI tracking systems and database.

3. Consults with clinicians, administrators, and QI teams on CQI activities such as chart reviews and accurate and complete documentation and coding, providing technical support and staff education as necessary. Ensures the gathering and analysis of QI data from every clinical department, converts data into statistics for analysis. Provides feedback in person and via reports to departments on trends and needed corrective actions. Leads QI committee, which regularly reviews QI data and prepares annual QI report. Resolves any patient complaints related to quality of care.

4. Develops mission, goals, and budgets for the QI department. Identifies QI opportunities, recognizes QI achievements, and recommends QI plan for next year.

5. Selects, trains, monitors, and evaluates department staff.

Education:	Bachelor's degree in health administration, science, or nursing. Master's degree in health care field preferred.
Experience:	Minimum five years of experience in health care setting including three years of management/QI experience.
Other Requirements:	Current RN or other clinical license as required. Current CPR certificate required.

Performance Requirements:	*Knowledge:*

1. Knowledge of QI philosophy, models, processes, and tools and their use in a health care setting. Familiar with ways to maintain currency with QI state-of-the-art and regulatory trends.
2. Knowledge of National Committee for Quality Assurance (NCQA) structure and standards and Healthplan Employer Data and Information Set (HEDIS) requirements and any accreditation standards.
3. Knowledge of how to use computerized statistical methods in CQI context.

Skills:

1. Skill in effective application of CQI teams, quality measures, clinical guidelines, and process management initiatives.
2. Skill in consistently meeting requirements of NCQA, HEDIS, and other regulators and accreditors.
3. Skill in using computer capabilities effectively to produce needed trend and evaluation data and documentation.

Abilities:

1. Ability to work effectively throughout medical practice by establishing effective working relationships with all departments and levels of staff.
2. Ability to present CQI concepts, methods, and tools in a clear and persuasive manner in verbal, written, automated, and audiovisual formats to variety of audiences.
3. Ability to promote the importance of QI concepts as related to the medical practice's mission and goals.

Equipment Operated:	Standard office equipment including computer hardware/software and training/presentation equipment such as audiovisual machinery.
Work Environment:	Office environment and occasional classroom. Well lighted and well ventilated. Rare contact with patients.
Mental/Physical Requirements:	Combination of sitting and standing. Occasional lifting/carrying of audiovisual equipment. Some stress related to high level of responsibility for quality care.

SPECIALTY JOB DESCRIPTIONS

- Audiologist
- Nurse Anesthetist
- Nurse Midwife
- Nutritionist
- Occupational Therapist
- Occupational Therapy Assistant
- Optician
- Optometrist
- Pharmacist
- Physical Therapist
- Physical Therapist Assistant
- Psychologist
- Respiratory Therapist
- Social Worker
- Speech-Language Pathologist/Therapist
- Surgical/Operating Technologist
- Volunteer Coordinator

Audiologist

Job Title: Audiologist

Department: Audiology or Clinical Services

Immediate Supervisor Title: Audiology Manager or Clinical Services Manager

Job Supervisory Responsibilities: None

General Summary: An exempt position responsible for providing primary care to patients who have hearing, balance, and related ear problems. They assist patients of all ages, often working closely with other clinicians. Hearing disorders can result from a variety of causes including trauma at birth, viral infections, genetic disorders, exposure to loud noise, certain medications, or aging.

Essential Job Responsibilities:

1. Examines patients to identify symptoms of hearing loss and other auditory, balance, and related sensory and neural problems.

2. Assesses the nature and extent of the problems using testing devices to measure the loudness at which a person begins to hear sounds and to distinguish between sounds. Assesses the impact of hearing loss on an individual's daily life.

3. Evaluates and diagnoses balance disorders, interprets results, and may coordinate treatment plan with medical, educational, and psychological information to make a diagnosis and determine a course of action.

4. Develops and implements hearing loss treatment plan, which may include cleaning the ear canal, fitting/dispensing hearing aids, and fitting/programming cochlear implants.

5. Counsels patients about hearing, balance, and related problems. Educates them about treatment plan including care and maintenance of hearing aids.

6. Documents patient condition and progress.

Education: Master's degree in audiology required. Clinical doctoral degree is expected to become the new standard.

Experience: Minimum three years of audiology experience, preferably in clinic setting.

Other Requirements: Most states regulate audiologists. Audiologists can acquire the certificate of clinical competence in audiology offered by the American Speech-Language Hearing Association, have 375 hours of supervised clinical experience, complete a 36-week postgraduate clinical fellowship, and pass the Praxis Series exam in audiology.

Performance Requirements: *Knowledge:*

1. Knowledge of mathematics, physics, chemistry, biology, psychology, and normal and abnormal communication.
2. Knowledge of anatomy, physiology, genetics, auditory, balance, and neural systems assessment and treatment, diagnosis and treatment, pharmacology, and ethics.
3. Knowledge of audiology equipment and measuring instruments.

Skills:

1. Skill in counseling on adjusting to hearing loss and teaching communication strategies.
2. Skill in developing special treatment programs on an individualized basis for hearing, balance, and neural issues.
3. Skill in recommending, fitting, and dispensing personal or large-area amplification systems and alerting devices.

Abilities:

1. Ability to communicate effectively with patients and families with particular emphasis on listening strategies.
2. Ability to collaborate appropriately with other clinicians to diagnose audiology problems and develop treatment plans.
3. Ability to gather patient information, analyze patient outcomes, pay attention to detail, and concentrate intensely.

Equipment Operated: Variety of testing instruments, hearing instruments, and computer equipment.

Work Environment: Audiologists usually work at a desk or table in clean, comfortable surroundings. Some exposure to communicable diseases and other conditions related to a clinic setting.

Mental/Physical Requirements: Occasionally required to use body mechanics including handling and lifting patients. May lift/carry items weighing up to 50 pounds. Normal visual acuity. Workload may cause stress at peak times.

Nurse Anesthetist

Job Title: Nurse Anesthetist

Department: Surgical Department, Obstetrics Department, or Clinical Services

Immediate Supervisor Title: Surgical Unit Manager

Job Supervisory Responsibilities: None

General Summary: An exempt position responsible for administering and monitoring anesthesia to patients during surgical and/or obstetrical procedures. Works closely with other health care professionals such as surgeons and anesthesiologists. Stays with patients for the entire procedure, constantly monitoring important body functions and individually modifying the anesthetic to ensure maximum safety and comfort.

Essential Job Responsibilities:

1. Examines and assesses patients before anesthesia including reviewing medical history and planning anesthesia delivery. Participates in preoperative teaching of patients, families, and staff on anesthesia aspects related to conditions and diseases. Reassures patient before procedure.

2. Prepares for anesthetic management. Ensures availability of required supplies and equipment before anesthetic procedure.

3. Administers various types of anesthesia to keep the patient pain free, including inhalational, intravenous, and regional anesthetics based on anesthetic plan and under direction of staff anesthesiologist. Performs any necessary invasive procedures including insertion of catheters.

4. Observes and records all patient functions being continuously monitored and evaluates need for ancillary drugs to maintain normal functioning.

5. Consults with staff anesthesiologist as necessary regarding patient's condition.

6. Documents results for patient record including all relevant assessment, care, and monitoring data.

7. Accompanies patient to recovery area to ensure condition is satisfactory. Oversees recovery from anesthesia. Follows the patient's postoperative course from recovery room to hospital room.

Education: BSN from accredited school of nursing. Successful completion of anesthesia program.

Experience: Minimum three years of nursing experience, with one year of acute care nursing experience and one to two years of experience as certified registered nurse anesthetist.

Other Requirements: Current RN state license. Current certification with the American Association of Nurse Anesthetists. Current CPR certificate.

Performance Requirements: *Knowledge:*

1. Knowledge of wide variety of anesthetics and procedures including spinal, intravenous, regional, and other techniques. Understands application of peripheral venous and radial arterial catheters. Stays current with new anesthesia trends.
2. Knowledge of Occupational Safety and Health Administration (OSHA) guidelines for collecting, disposing of, and working with contaminated or possibly infectious materials and specimens.
3. Knowledge of anatomy, physiology, pathophysiology, biochemistry, chemistry, physics, and pharmacology.

Skills:

1. Skill in administering anesthetic doses to broad range of patients.
2. Skill in performing variety of anesthetic techniques proficiently.
3. Skill in educating patients, families, and staff on procedures.

Abilities:

1. Ability to communicate effectively and participate collaboratively on health care team.
2. Ability to respond appropriately in emergencies including using CPR.
3. Ability to demonstrate full range of body motion, manual/finger dexterity, and eye–hand coordination.

Equipment Operated: Wide range of anesthetic equipment and supplies.

Work Environment: Surgical unit setting. Frequent exposure to infectious, communicable disease situations, toxic substances, medicinal preparations, and other conditions common in clinic setting.

Mental/Physical Requirements: Standing up to six to eight hours per day. Requires ability to lift/move up to 50 pounds of equipment and supplies. High level of stress related to high level of responsibility.

Nurse Midwife

Job Title:	Nurse Midwife
Department:	Obstetrics, Women's Health, or Clinical Services
Immediate Supervisor Title:	Manager of OB/GYN, Women's Health, or Clinical Services
Job Supervisory Responsibilities:	None
General Summary:	An exempt position responsible for providing prenatal education and support, attending childbirth, providing encouragement during labor and delivery, and supervising the general care of women and children directly after birth. Provides care to women during normal pregnancies and deliveries and calls on obstetricians or other physicians if complications develop.

Essential Job Responsibilities:

1. Performs the nursing duties related to midwifery including gynecological exams, preconception care, prenatal care, labor and delivery care, care after birth, newborn care, disease prevention, family planning, health maintenance counseling, and menopausal management.

2. Educates women about different types of care available and encourages them to enhance their pregnancy by being involved. Emphasizes patient education, active participation, clear communication between the provider and the woman, and an individualized health care experience. Advocates birth education, natural childbirth, and the participation of the entire family. Relies on technology only when medically necessary. Writes prescriptions as needed.

3. Serves as OB/GYN team member working closely with physicians and other staff to ensure healthy pregnancies and deliveries. Provides emotional and social support, which can reduce the length of labor, the need for pain medication, the likelihood for use of forceps or other operative devices during delivery, or the possibility of cesarean delivery.

4. Oversees the medical care of assigned pregnant patients under the supervision of a physician. Provides support to mother and family.

5. Teaches patients about elements of mother–baby bonding, protecting from inadequate heat, overstimulation, noisy/brightly lit environments, cuddling/hugging, recognizing signs of infant pain/discomfort, and breast feeding.

Education:	BSN and successful completion of nurse midwifery program accredited by the American College of Nurse Midwives (ACNM).
Experience:	Minimum three years of experience as RN; one year as midwife, preferably in medical practice setting.
Other Requirements:	Current RN state license. Current CPR certificate. Certification by state as a certified nurse midwife. Certification by ACNM, including meeting recommended ACNM continuing competency requirements and passing the national certification examination.

Performance Requirements: *Knowledge:*

1. Knowledge of nurse midwifery principles and techniques.
2. Knowledge of methods ensuring safe working environment for patient, family, and staff including using appropriate personal protection equipment.
3. Knowledge of theories of family dynamics, mother–child attachment, parenting, and adult learning concepts.

Skills:

1. Skill in midwifery through appropriate prenatal education and support, coaching during pregnancy and delivery.
2. Skill in showing parents how to use distraction techniques to calm baby, deal with sibling rivalry, practice effective parenting techniques.
3. Skill in showing other staff how to best help pregnant/postpartum women by effective teaching of principles and methods.

Abilities:

1. Ability to demonstrate full range of motion, eye–hand coordination, and manual/finger dexterity.
2. Ability to assess a situation, consider alternatives, and choose an appropriate course of action.
3. Ability to participate effectively as a team member.

Equipment Operated: Standard OB/GYN equipment for examining and caring for patient during pregnancy and delivery.

Work Environment: Combination of office, exam, and birthing rooms. Frequent exposure to communicable diseases, toxic substances, medicinal preparations, and other conditions common to a medical practice environment.

Mental/Physical Requirements: Varied activities including sitting, standing, walking, bending, reaching, and lifting. Occasionally lifts and carries items weighing up to 100 pounds. Stress related to dealing with anxious patients and responsibility for baby and mother.

Nutritionist

Job Title: Nutritionist

Department: Clinical Services

Immediate Supervisor Title: Clinical Services Manager

Job Supervisory Responsibilities: None

General Summary: An exempt position responsible for nutrition assessment, counseling, education, and program evaluation.

Essential Job Responsibilities:

1. Assesses client medical history, including nutritional status, diet history, and food habits. Conducts individual sessions to discuss patient's nutritional needs and determine risk factors. Confers with physician and other clinicians as appropriate on effect of nutritional status.

2. Develops nutritional plan for patient, presents information to patient/family individually about implementing nutrition plan including recommendations for special diets and diet techniques to ensure proper preparation and nutritional intake.

3. Documents dietary assessment/plan summary for medical record.

4. Conducts patient education programs for weight reduction, cultural preferences, and special-need diets for certain health conditions such as diabetes, high blood pressure, etc. Teaches correct food preparation and safe food handling. Conducts nutritional health education programs for staff.

5. Acts as liaison with food access and subsidy programs. Participates collaboratively with other providers and resources to assess and address health issues including the development of community standards and programs.

Education: Bachelor's degree in nutrition, food service, or community health. Master's degree preferred.

Experience: Minimum three years of experience as dietitian. Two years of experience in health setting as dietitian/patient educator preferred.

Other Requirements: Registered dietitian as certified by the American Dietetic Association.

Performance Requirements: *Knowledge:*

1. Knowledge of theoretical and practical principles related to nutrition and dietetics.
2. Knowledge of medical terminology, universal precautions and food sanitation/safety procedures, and federal/state regulations related to food preparation, storage, etc.
3. Knowledge of ethnic eating patterns and cultural customs related to food.
4. Knowledge of education principles including human behavior and behavior modification techniques and presentation methods.

Skills:

1. Skill in nutrition assessment.
2. Skill in problem-solving and handling crisis situations.
3. Skill in utilizing behavioral modification techniques to improve patient nutritional status.
4. Skill in developing and presenting patient/staff/community education workshops.

Abilities:

1. Ability to read and follow written and oral medical orders.
2. Ability to analyze medical condition and make appropriate judgments about dietary issues.
3. Ability to work effectively in collaborative clinical and community situations.

Equipment Operated: Standard office equipment, including computer.

Work Environment: Combination of office, exam rooms, and classrooms. May be exposed to communicable diseases and other conditions common to clinic setting.

Mental/Physical Requirements: Varied activities including sitting, walking, reaching, bending, and lifting. Must be able to stand two to four hours during educational sessions. Occasionally required to carry equipment and supplies weighing up to 50 pounds. Low level of stress.

Occupational Therapist

Job Title:	Occupational Therapist
Department:	Rehabilitation Therapy Department or Clinical Services Department
Immediate Supervisor Title:	Rehabilitation Therapy Manager or Clinical Services Manager
Job Supervisory Responsibilities:	May participate in supervision of occupational therapy assistants
General Summary:	An exempt position responsible for helping patients improve their ability to perform tasks in their daily living and working environments. Patients may have conditions that are mentally, physically, developmentally, or emotionally disabling.

Essential Job Responsibilities:

1. Assesses patients and develops treatment plans in collaboration with physicians and other clinicians.

2. Assists patients to develop, recover, or maintain daily living and work skills. Helps patients to improve their basic motor functions and reasoning ability and to compensate for any permanent loss of function to reach the goal of having independent, productive, and satisfying lives.

3. Helps patients in performing a variety of activities from operating a computer to dealing with daily needs such as dressing, cooking, and eating.

4. Assists patients with exercises that increase strength and dexterity, visual acuity, and the ability to discern patterns.

5. Uses variety of equipment during treatment including computer programs to help patients improve decision making, abstract reasoning, problem solving, perceptual skills, memory, sequencing, and coordination to aid in independent living.

6. Teaches patients, particularly those with permanent disabilities such as spinal cord injuries, cerebral palsy, or muscular dystrophy, in the use of adaptive equipment including wheelchairs, orthotics, and aids for eating and dressing.

7. Follows medical practice policies related to compliance, safety, and infection control. Documents patient treatment and outcomes in medical record.

Education:	Bachelor's degree in occupational therapy from accredited school plus master's degree in field (new requirement as of 2007).
Experience:	Minimum two years of experience, preferably in clinic setting.
Other Requirements:	Current state occupational therapist license, successful completion of national certification examination. Current CPR certificate.

Performance Requirements: *Knowledge:*

1. Knowledge of occupational therapy principles, standards, and applications.
2. Knowledge of physical, biological, and behavioral sciences as well as application of occupational therapy equipment, devices, and patient-specific therapeutic devices. Understanding of how to modify equipment as needed.
3. Knowledge of clinic policies and regulations related to infection control, safety, and quality improvement.

Skills:

1. Skill in evaluating and treating patients.
2. Skill in proper use of occupational therapy equipment and devices.
3. Skill in assessing and recording patient activities and progress.

Abilities:

1. Ability to collaborate with patients, families, and employers to modify workplace or home environment in line with patient's condition, including identification of environmental factors and hazards.
2. Ability to communicate with patients and families in caring and compassionate manner to encourage behavioral changes.
3. Ability to analyze patient data and behavior and modify treatment plan as appropriate.

Equipment Operated: Variety of therapeutic equipment including wheelchairs, orthotics, and aids for activities of daily living. Computer hardware and software for record keeping.

Work Environment: Exam, treatment, and exercise rooms. May also occasionally require visits to patient homes and workplaces. Exposure to communicable diseases, biohazards, and conditions related to clinic setting.

Mental/Physical Requirements: Extensive physical activities including standing, stooping, lifting, bending, and twisting. Must be able to transport/transfer patient safely. Occasional need to lift/carry and move equipment and supplies weighing up to 50 pounds. Some stress related to dealing with concerns of patients and families.

Occupational Therapy Assistant

Job Title: Occupational Therapy Assistant

Department: Rehabilitation Therapy or Clinical Services

Immediate Supervisor Title: Occupational Therapy Manager or Rehabilitation Therapy Manager. May also be supervised by occupational therapists (OTs) and physicians.

Job Supervisory Responsibilities: None

General Summary: A nonexempt position responsible for assisting OTs in assessing and treating patients to provide rehabilitative services to persons with mental, physical, emotional, or developmental impairments. OT assistant has more training and responsibility than aide.

Essential Job Responsibilities:
1. Helps implements plans to improve patients' quality of life and ability to perform daily activities. Prepares materials and assembles equipment used during treatments.
2. Helps injured patients to deal with activities of daily living at home and/or to re-enter the labor force by teaching them to compensate for lost motor skills. Helps individuals increase their independence.
3. Assists with rehabilitative activities and exercises outlined in a treatment plan developed by an OT. Activities may include teaching the proper method of moving from a bed to a wheelchair to the best way to stretch and limber the muscles of the hand.
4. Assists in helping to modify the plan to better fit the patient's condition and achieve improved results.
5. Helps OT document for the medical record and other paperwork.
6. Prepares and cleans equipment, orders supplies, follows infection control and safety procedures. Handles clerical tasks such as scheduling appointments, answering the phone, ordering/stocking supplies.

Education: High school diploma. Associate's degree or a certificate from an accredited school for assistant. OT aide on-the-job training acceptable.

Experience: Minimum one year of experience as OT assistant/aide, preferably in clinic setting.

Other Requirements: Most states regulate occupational therapist assistants and they must pass a national certification exam after they graduate. Passing the test earns them the title of certified occupational therapy assistant. Current CPR certificate.

Performance Requirements:	*Knowledge:*
	1. Knowledge of physiology, biology, and body mechanics.
	2. Knowledge of OT procedures and equipment.
	3. Knowledge of safety, infection control, and quality improvement policies and procedures.

Knowledge:

1. Knowledge of physiology, biology, and body mechanics.
2. Knowledge of OT procedures and equipment.
3. Knowledge of safety, infection control, and quality improvement policies and procedures.

Skills:

1. Skill in using OT equipment properly and safely to transfer/transport and treat patients.
2. Skill in observing and recording patient progress or concerns.
3. Skill in helping patients with rehabilitative activities and exercises.

Abilities:

1. Ability to encourage patients to achieve treatment plan goals.
2. Ability to interact effectively with patients, families, and clinical team.
3. Ability to demonstrate eye–hand coordination, manual/finger dexterity, and agility.

Equipment Operated: May operate variety of OT devices during exercise and treatment as well as patient assistive devices such as wheelchairs, canes, reachers, and dressing/eating aids.

Work Environment: Combination of exam, treatment, and exercise rooms. Exposure to communicable diseases, biohazards, and other conditions related to clinic setting.

Mental/Physical Requirements: Extensive physical demands including walking, standing, lifting, bending, twisting, and stooping. Occasional heavy lifting when transporting/transferring patient. May lift/carry up to 100+ pounds of equipment. Some stress from dealing with anxious patients.

Optician

Job Title:	Optician
Department:	Optical or Clinical Services
Immediate Supervisor Title:	Optical Manager, Optometrist, or Clinical Services Manager
Job Supervisory Responsibilities:	May supervise optical technicians
General Summary:	An exempt position responsible for dispensing eyeglasses and contact lenses, following prescriptions written by ophthalmologists or optometrists.

Essential Job Responsibilities:

1. Examines written prescriptions to determine the specifications of lenses.

2. Recommends eyeglass frames, lenses, and lens coatings or contact lenses after considering the prescription and the patient's occupation, habits, and facial features.

3. Measures patients' eyes, including the distance between the centers of the pupils and the distance between the ocular surface and the lens. Selects the type of contact lens material if this type of corrective device is chosen.

4. Duplicates eyeglasses by using a focimeter to record eyeglass measurements. May obtain patient's previous record in order to re-make eyeglasses or contact lenses or may verify prescription with the examining optometrist or ophthalmologist.

5. Prepares work orders, including prescriptions for eyeglass lenses and information on their size, material, color, and style that give ophthalmic laboratory technician the information needed to grind and insert lenses into a frame. Prepares work order for contact lenses with similar information.

6. Verifies that the lenses have been ground to specifications. May reshape or bend the eyeglass frame by hand or by using pliers so that the eyeglasses fit the patient properly and comfortably. May fix, adjust, and refit broken frames.

7. Instructs patients about adapting to, wearing, and caring for eyeglasses. Instructs, often during several visits, patients on inserting, removing, and caring for contacts.

8. Documents patient care and treatment. Follows safety, infection control, and quality assurance protocols.

Education:	High school diploma, some college or postsecondary optical training preferred. On-the-job training or two- to four-year apprenticeships often provided.
Experience:	Minimum three years of clinical experience, preferably in optical laboratory or department.
Other Requirements:	Some states require that dispensing opticians be licensed. Some states also may require applicants to pass a state practical exam, state written exam, or certification exam offered by the American Board of Opticianry and the National Contact Lens Examiners.

Performance Requirements: *Knowledge:*

1. Knowledge of physics, basic anatomy, algebra, and trigonometry.
2. Knowledge of optical equipment and instruments.
3. Knowledge of safety, infection control, documentation, and quality improvement protocols.

Skills:

1. Skill in using computers for optical mathematics and optical physics.
2. Skill in using precision measuring instruments and other optical machinery and tools.
3. Skill in adjusting eyeglasses/contact lenses to best fit patients.

Abilities:

1. Ability to follow prescriptions and patient information to develop accurate work orders for ophthalmic lab technicians to make eyeglasses and contact lenses.
2. Ability to collaborate effectively with optical clinical team.
3. Ability to demonstrate eye–hand coordination, manual/finger dexterity, agility, and color vision and depth perception with visual acuity correctable to 20/25 while fitting eyeglasses and contacts.

Equipment Operated: Variety of optical equipment and instruments including focimeters, pliers, and computer hardware/software.

Work Environment: Medical office, exam and laboratory setting. Well-lighted and well-ventilated surroundings. May be exposed to communicable diseases and other conditions related to clinic setting.

Mental/Physical Requirements: Combination of standing, sitting, walking, stooping, bending, and reaching. Occasionally must lift/carry up to 50 pounds. Low level of stress.

Optometrist

Job Title:	Optometrist
Department:	Optical or Clinical Services
Immediate Supervisor Title:	Optical or Clinical Services Manager
Job Supervisory Responsibilities:	May supervise opticians and optical technicians
General Summary:	An exempt position responsible for providing primary vision care via examination, testing, prescribing, vision therapy, and low-vision rehabilitation.
Essential Job Responsibilities:	1. Examines patients' eyes to diagnose vision problems and eye diseases; tests patients' visual acuity, depth and color perception, and ability to focus and coordinate the eyes. Reviews medical history. Diagnoses conditions caused by systemic diseases such as diabetes and high blood pressure, referring patients to other health practitioners as needed.
	2. Analyzes test results and develops a treatment plan.
	3. Prescribes/administers drugs to patients to aid in the diagnosis and treatment of vision problems.
	4. Prescribes eyeglasses and contact lenses. Utilizes vision therapeutic techniques and rehabilitation techniques for those with low vision.
	5. Documents patient condition and progress.
	6. Follows infection control, safety, and quality improvement policies.
Education:	Bachelor's degree with preoptometric science studies preferred. Doctor of optometry degree from an accredited optometry school required.
Experience:	Minimum three years of experience as optometrist, with at least one year in a medical practice preferred.
Other Requirements:	All states require that optometrists be licensed. Degreed applicants must pass both a written National Board examination and a national, regional, or state clinic board examination. Some states also may require applicants to pass an exam on relevant state laws. Licenses are renewed every one to three years and continuing education credits are needed for renewal.

Performance Requirements: *Knowledge:*

1. Knowledge of mathematics, physics, chemistry, and biology.
2. Knowledge of health and visual sciences, diagnosis and treatment of eye disorders.
3. Knowledge of pharmacology, optics, vision science, biochemistry, and systemic disease.

Skills:

1. Skill in developing and implementing ways to protect eyes.
2. Skill in diagnosing vision problems and diseases.
3. Skill in diagnosing other health conditions that cause eye-related symptoms.

Abilities:

1. Ability to deal tactfully with patients, families, and other clinicians.
2. Ability to pay attention to detail.
3. Ability to demonstrate manual/finger dexterity, agility, eye–hand coordination, and color vision and depth perception with visual acuity correctable to 20/25.

Equipment Operated: Optical machinery and instruments. Computer hardware and software for documentation.

Work Environment: Office, laboratory, and exam rooms. Well lighted, well ventilated, clean and comfortable. Some exposure to communicable diseases and other conditions related to clinic settings.

Mental/Physical Requirements: Combination of sitting, standing, walking, stooping, bending, and reaching. Occasionally must lift/carry up to 50 pounds. Periodic stress related to workload and managerial responsibilities.

Pharmacist

Job Title:	Pharmacist
Department:	Pharmacy
Immediate Supervisor Title:	Pharmacy Manager or Manager of Clinical Services.
Job Supervisory Responsibilities:	May participate in the supervision of pharmacy technicians
General Summary:	An exempt, licensed pharmacist position responsible for safely filling and dispensing prescriptions in clinic setting.

Essential Job Responsibilities:

1. Fills and dispenses prescriptions ordered by clinic physicians according to appropriate protocols for preparing products suitable for patient use including checking patient profiles for incompatible orders and discussing with physicians.

2. Maintains paper/automated prescription record for each patient and updates with appropriate documentation. Monitors drug therapy periodically by evaluating patient medical history for significant drug interactions, adverse reactions, therapeutic drug dosages, and compliance with prescription orders.

3. Provides drug education to patients/families including information on drug interactions. Educates staff via in-service presentations, medical literature searches, and individual consulting. Acts as preceptor for pharmacy and pharmacy technician students.

4. Participates in quality improvement efforts related to drug use management under supervision of pharmacy manager or clinical services manager.

5. Participates in inventory control under the direction of pharmacy manager or clinical services manager, including purchasing, receiving, and stocking medication and pharmacy supplies. Complies with governmental and other regulations related to preparation, packaging, and/storage of products.

Education:	Bachelor's degree in pharmacy, master's degree preferred. Certificate from accredited school of pharmacy.
Experience:	Minimum of three years experience as pharmacist, preferably in clinic setting.
Other Requirements:	Current state pharmacy license.

Performance Requirements: *Knowledge:*

1. Knowledge of disease states, therapeutic use of drugs, clinically significant drug interactions, and adverse drug reactions and their interrelatedness.
2. Knowledge of drug names, strength, dosage forms, generic equivalent, and storage requirements.
3. Knowledge of basic pharmacy compounding/dispensing.
4. Knowledge of inventory control procedures and practices.
5. Knowledge of state laws and regulations regarding the practice of pharmacy.

Skills:

1. Skill in working in team environment and with public.
2. Skill in data entry and basic computer usage.
3. Skill in using analytical, problem-solving, organizational, and communication techniques.

Abilities:

1. Ability to analyze and interpret patient history and physician orders and to problem solve accurately.
2. Ability to communicate technical knowledge to patients and staff in user-friendly manner.
3. Ability to make mathematical calculations to determine compounding and prescription amounts.
4. Ability to coordinate eye–hand movements and to use manual dexterity.

Equipment Operated: Standard pharmacy items such as packaging and dispensing equipment.

Work Environment: Pharmacy and medical office settings. Frequent contact with public. Occasional exposure to communicable diseases, toxic substances, medicinal preparations, and other conditions common to a pharmacy.

Mental/Physical Requirements: Stands up to eight hours per day, bending, stooping, twisting, and reaching. Occasional stress from dealing with heavy workload.

Physical Therapist

Job Title:	Physical Therapist
Department:	Rehabilitation Therapy or Clinical Services
Immediate Supervisor Title:	Rehabilitation Therapy Manager and/or Clinical Services Manager
Job Supervisory Responsibilities:	May participate in supervising physical therapy assistants
General Summary:	An exempt position responsible for rehabilitating persons with physical disabilities. Patients include accident victims and individuals with disabling conditions such as back pain, arthritis, heart disease, fractures, head injuries, and neurological conditions such as multiple sclerosis. May specialize in pediatrics, geriatrics, orthopedics, sports medicine, neurology, or cardiopulmonary physical therapy.

Essential Job Responsibilities:

1. Helps to restore physical function, improve mobility, relieve pain, and prevent permanent disability. Assists in restoring, maintaining, and promoting overall fitness and health.

2. Examines patients' medical histories. Tests and measures patients' strength, range of motion, balance and coordination, posture, muscle performance, respiration, and motor function.

3. Determines patients' ability to be independent and reintegrate into the workplace or community after injury or illness.

4. Develops plans describing a treatment strategy, its purposes, and its anticipated outcome. Plan often includes exercise regimens at the clinic and at home to increase flexibility, strength, or endurance. May use electrical stimulation, hot packs, cold compresses, and ultrasound to relieve pain and reduce swelling.

5. Teaches patients how to use assistive and adaptive devices such as crutches, prostheses, and wheelchairs.

6. Documents patients' progress, conducts periodic examinations, and modifies treatments with emphasis on identification of areas requiring more/less attention.

Education:	Bachelor's degree in physical therapy from accredited program; successful completion of clinical internship. Master's degree in physical therapy preferred.
Experience:	Minimum two years of experience as a physical therapist, preferably in clinic setting.
Other Requirements:	Current state physical therapist license. Current CPR certificate.

Performance Requirements: *Knowledge:*

1. Knowledge of basic science including biology, chemistry, and physics as well as biomechanics, neuroanatomy, and disease manifestations.
2. Knowledge of medical practice policies/procedures, regulations, safety/injection control, and quality assurance requirements.
3. Knowledge of examination techniques and therapeutic procedures.

Skills:

1. Skill in appropriate evaluation and treatment of patients including hands-on procedures such as deep-tissue massage.
2. Skill in using physical therapy equipment by consistently using devices appropriately to improve patient health status.
3. Skill in effectively maintaining equipment; successful completion of related competency testing.

Abilities:

1. Ability to effectively communicate interpersonally in order to educate patients about their physical therapy treatments.
2. Ability to demonstrate compassion and desire to help patients.
3. Ability to analyze data and modify treatment plans as appropriate.

Equipment Operated: Often demonstrates and helps patients use assistive and adaptive devices such as wheelchairs, walkers, crutches, and canes. Operates physical therapy equipment such as ultrasound, traction, and electrical stimulation.

Work Environment: Medical office, exam rooms, and specially equipped therapy facilities. Exposure to communicable diseases, toxic substances, and biohazards.

Mental/Physical Requirements: Often have to stoop, kneel, crouch, lift, and stand for long periods. Frequently move heavy equipment, lift patients or help them turn, stand or walk. Occasionally must be able to lift and carry 50+ pounds. Periodic stress from workload or anxious patients.

Physical Therapist Assistant

Job Title: Physical Therapist Assistant

Department: Rehabilitation Therapy or Clinical Services

Immediate Supervisor Title: Rehabilitation Manager or Physical Therapy Manager; may be supervised by physical therapists (PTs) or physicians

Job Supervisory Responsibilities: None

General Summary: A nonexempt position responsible for performing specific nonclinical physical therapy procedures and related tasks under the direction of a physical therapist. Assistants have more training and responsibility than aides.

Essential Job Responsibilities:
1. Assists PTs in providing services that help improve mobility, relieve pain, and prevent or limit permanent physical disabilities of patients suffering from injuries from accidents or from diseases such as arthritis, cerebral palsy, or heart disease.
2. Helps PTs fulfill patient treatment plan and procedures such as exercises, massages, electrical stimulation, paraffin baths, hot and cold packs, traction, and ultrasound.
3. Records patient responses to treatments and reports outcomes of each treatment to the physical therapist.
4. Keeps treatment area clean and organized in preparation for each patient's therapy.
5. Helps patients moving to/from treatment area by pushing them in wheelchairs or providing support during ambulation.
6. Performs some clerical tasks such as ordering supplies, answering the phone, and completing paperwork.

Education: High school diploma preferred. Successful completion of physical therapist assistant program of accredited school. On-the-job-training acceptable for physical therapist aides.

Experience: Minimum one year of experience, preferably in clinic setting.

Other Requirements: Some states require licensure/registration for a physical therapy assistant. Current CPR certificate.

Performance Requirements: *Knowledge:*

1. Knowledge of how to carry out treatment plans as prescribed by physician and developed by physical therapist.
2. Knowledge of operating therapeutic equipment and devices including crutches, walkers, exercise apparatus, canes, electrical stimulators, traction, and heat/cold modalities.
3. Knowledge of documentation of care and other patient information for medical record including history, treatment, and consultations.

Skills:

1. Skill in assisting with exam/exercise room cleanliness, equipment maintenance, and supply ordering/inventorying/stocking.
2. Skill in complying with policies/procedures related to infection control, safety, and quality improvement.
3. Skill in using assistive devices effectively to aid patients.

Abilities:

1. Ability to communicate clearly with staff, patient, and families.
2. Ability to observe patients and report outcomes and concerns to PT.
3. Ability to follow instructions carefully when assisting clients.

Equipment Operated: Variety of exam/treatment/exercise equipment including assistive devices such as wheelchairs and treatment equipment such as traction devices. Use of computer for record keeping and documentation.

Work Environment: Primarily treatment and exercise rooms. Exposure to communicable diseases, biohazards, and other conditions related to medical setting.

Mental/Physical Requirements: High level of physical demands including standing, walking, lifting, bending, and stooping. Helps lift, carry, and move equipment weighing up to 100 pounds. Must be able to transfer/transport patient safely. Occasional stress during heavy workload peaks.

Psychologist

Job Title:	Psychologist
Department:	Clinical Services or Counseling/Mental Health Department
Immediate Supervisor Title:	Clinical Services Manager or Mental Health Department Manager
Job Supervisory Responsibilities:	None
General Summary:	An exempt position responsible for providing mental health assessment and counseling to patients.

Essential Job Responsibilities:

1. Provides consultation to physicians and nurses about special-need referrals. Assists with early identification of psychological disorders.

2. Observes patients in various situations. Conducts psychological testing and mental status evaluations, identifies areas of concern, makes independent diagnoses, and initiates mental health care and follow-up. Develops treatment plans.

3. Writes reports on mental status evaluations, treatment plans, medications prescribed, patient progress, and other issues.

4. Screens and documents patient use of prescribed medications and adherence to medical advice.

5. Plans and implements quality improvement programs to support department goals and meet accreditation requirements.

Education:	Doctorate degree in clinical psychology.
Experience:	Minimum two years of post-doctoral degree experience in the direct evaluation and treatment of patients with mental disorders, under the supervision of a licensed mental health professional.
Other Requirements:	State license in psychology.

Performance Requirements: *Knowledge:*

1. Knowledge of diagnosis and treatment of mental health disorders. Advanced study of mental health assessment practices, regulations, and laws relating to clinical psychology practice. Understanding of principles of legal documentation and medical records release of information.

2. Knowledge of psychological test administration, scoring, and interpretation.

3. Knowledge of psychotropic medications and treatment uses.

4. Knowledge of community mental health service delivery systems and other resources.

Skills:

1. Skill in triage, mental health diagnostics, and treatment.

2. Skill in psychological and behavioral intervention.

3. Skill in working with diverse patients.

Abilities:

1. Ability to analyze patient data and apply psychologically relevant methodologies and techniques.

2. Ability to work sensitively with variety of personalities.

3. Ability to work with research and testing data to develop diagnosis.

Equipment Operated: Standard office equipment, particularly computer hardware and software.

Work Environment: Office setting; well-lighted and well-ventilated, adequate space.

Mental/Physical Requirements: Mostly sedentary. Some standing. Occasional stress from patient workload. Complex cases may cause stress.

Respiratory Therapist

Job Title:	Respiratory Therapist
Department:	Rehabilitation Therapy, Pulmonology, or Clinical Services
Immediate Supervisor Title:	Rehabilitation Therapy Manager, Pulmonology Manager, or Clinical Services Manager
Job Supervisory Responsibilities:	May supervise respiratory therapy technicians
General Summary:	An exempt position responsible for evaluating, treating, and caring for patients with breathing or other cardiopulmonary disorders under the direction of a physician. Therapists have more responsibility than technicians.

Essential Job Responsibilities:

1. Evaluates and treats all types of patients, ranging from premature infants whose lungs are not fully developed to elderly people whose lungs are diseased. Interviews patients and performs limited physical examinations.

2. Conducts diagnostic tests including checking breathing capacity and determining the concentration of oxygen and other gases in patients' blood. Measures patients' pH, which indicates the acidity or alkalinity of the blood.

3. Treats patients using oxygen or oxygen mixtures, chest physiotherapy, and aerosol medications. May use oxygen mask or nasal cannula on the patient and set the oxygen flow at the level prescribed by the physician.

4. Performs chest physiotherapy on patients to remove mucus from their lungs and make it easier for them to breathe. Administers aerosols, which are liquid medications suspended in a gas that forms a mist that is inhaled. Teaches patients how to inhale the aerosol properly to ensure its effectiveness.

5. Teaches patients and their families to use ventilators and other life-support systems at home. May visit patients at home to inspect and clean equipment and to ensure its proper use.

6. Complies with safety, infection control, and quality improvement policies and practices. Documents patient care for medical records.

Education:	Associate's degree or bachelor's degree in respiratory therapy or cardiopulmonary technology from an accredited school required.
Experience:	Minimum one year of respiratory therapy experience in acute care setting required. Minimum six months of experience in diagnostic testing required. Minimum six months of medical practice experience preferred.
Other Requirements:	Most states require respiratory therapists to obtain a license. Passing the certified respiratory therapist exam qualifies respiratory therapists for state licenses.

Performance Requirements: *Knowledge:*

1. Knowledge of human anatomy, physiology, pathophysiology, chemistry, physics, microbiology, pharmacology, and mathematics.

2. Knowledge of therapeutic and diagnostic procedures and tests, equipment, patient assessment, and cardiopulmonary resuscitation.

3. Knowledge of techniques for teaching patients how to care for themselves outside of clinic.

Skills:

1. Skill in applying clinical practice guidelines, cardiac and pulmonary rehabilitation, respiratory health promotion, and disease prevention.

2. Skill in medical record keeping to measure patient progress.

3. Skill in safe use of respiratory therapy equipment including adherence to safety precautions and regular maintenance and testing of equipment to minimize the risk of injury

Abilities:

1. Ability to teach patients and families about using respiratory therapy equipment and techniques at home and in other nonclinical locales.

2. Ability to collaborate effectively with physicians and other clinicians.

3. Ability to deal compassionately with anxious patients who may have life-threatening illnesses.

Equipment Operated: Variety of respiratory therapy equipment including oxygen equipment, ventilators, pulmonary measurement instruments, blood draw equipment, and suction equipment.

Work Environment: Various laboratory, exam, and office settings. Trained to work with hazardous gases stored under pressure. Exposure to communicable diseases, biohazards, and other conditions related to clinical environment.

Mental/Physical Requirements: Long hours involving standing, bending, and walking. May have to deal with stressful emergency situations. Occasional need to lift/carry up to 50 pounds. Some stress related to dealing with anxious patients.

Social Worker

Job Title:	Social Worker
Department:	Clinical Services or Mental Health
Immediate Supervisor Title:	Clinical Services Manager or Mental Health Department Manager
Job Supervisory Responsibilities:	None
General Summary:	An exempt position responsible for providing professional social work services to patients and families including direct counseling services, crisis intervention, and coordination of community services/resources. Performance of duties may be autonomous and self-directed as part of an interdisciplinary team.
Essential Job Responsibilities:	1. Conducts comprehensive, culturally sensitive psychosocial assessments, develops care plans, and provides counseling and crisis intervention services to individuals and families.
	2. Coordinates services with appropriate clinic and community resources.
	3. Provides information and education about health/mental health issues to individual patients and to groups.
	4. Documents assessment, intervention, and treatment data in medical record.
	5. Provides social work consultation to clinic staff and community providers as appropriate. Serves as liaison to community health care network.
Education:	Master's degree in social work from accredited school of social work. Additional course work in area of specialty (e.g., psychiatric, pediatric, geriatric) preferred.
Experience:	Minimum two years of experience in social work and broad background with diverse patient populations, preferably in medical setting. Additional one year of experience in area of specialty preferred.
Other Requirements:	Registered to practice social work in state and/or a current state social work license.

Performance Requirements: *Knowledge:*

1. Knowledge of professional social work principles, methodology, and ethics and of human psychosocial development within the family, community, and culture.

2. Knowledge of the use of therapeutic relationship to foster patient involvement. Familiarity with brief therapy theories/techniques and therapeutic process. Understanding of techniques for facilitating client motivation to change behavior.

3. Knowledge of health and social issues impacting diverse clients and their well-being.

Skills:

1. Skill in crisis intervention.

2. Skill in client advocacy.

3. Skill in case management.

Abilities:

1. Ability to interact effectively as member of interdisciplinary health care team.

2. Ability to identify and utilize community resources.

3. Ability to communicate appropriately with diverse patient population.

Equipment Operated: Standard office equipment including computer hardware and software to access community resource database.

Work Environment: Office and exam room settings. Some exposure to communicable diseases. Some interactions in community provider network/settings.

Mental/Physical Requirements: Combination of sitting, standing, and walking. Occasional stress in balancing multiple demands and in dealing with patients/families experiencing tension.

Speech-Language Pathologist/Therapist

Job Title:	Speech-Language Pathologist/Therapist
Department:	Rehabilitation Therapy, Audiology, or Clinical Services
Immediate Supervisor Title:	Rehabilitation Therapy Manager, Clinical Services Manager, or Audiology Department Manager
Job Supervisory Responsibilities:	None
General Summary:	An exempt position responsible for helping to treat and prevent speech, language, cognitive-communication, voice, swallowing, fluency, and other related disorders. Such disorders may result from stroke, brain injury or deterioration, developmental delays or disorders, learning disabilities, cerebral palsy, cleft palate, voice pathology, mental retardation, hearing loss, or emotional problems.

Essential Job Responsibilities:

1. Assesses patients who cannot produce speech sounds or cannot produce them clearly; those with speech rhythm and fluency problems such as stuttering; people with voice disorders such as inappropriate pitch or harsh voice; those with problems understanding and producing language; those who wish to improve their communication skills by modifying an accent; those with cognitive communication impairments such as attention, memory, and problem-solving disorders; and those with swallowing difficulties.

2. Uses qualitative and quantitative assessment methods, including standardized tests, as well as special instruments, to analyze and diagnose the nature and extent of speech, language, and swallowing impairments, which may be congenital, developmental, or acquired.

3. Develops an individualized plan of care that is tailored to each patient's needs. May use augmentative or alternative communication, including automated devices and sign language, with individuals with little or no speech capability.

4. Educates individuals with speech-language difficulties on how to make sounds, improve their voices, or increase their oral or written language skills to communicate more effectively.

5. Teaches individuals with swallowing difficulties how to strengthen muscles or use compensatory strategies to swallow without choking or inhaling food or liquid.

6. Keeps records on patient initial evaluation progress and discharge. Counsels patients and families concerning communication disorders.

Education:	Master's degree in speech-language pathology from accredited school. Supervised clinical training in communication disorders.
Experience:	Minimum two years of experience as speech therapist, preferably in clinic setting.
Other Requirements:	Current state license as speech-language pathologist. Passing score on the national exam on speech-language pathology, offered through the Praxis Series of the Educational Testing Service.

Performance Requirements: *Knowledge:*

1. Knowledge of anatomy, physiology, and the development of the areas of the body involved in speech, language, and swallowing.

2. Knowledge of the nature of disorders, acoustics, and psychological aspects of communication. Understanding of how to evaluate and treat speech, language, and swallowing disorders.

3. Knowledge of clinical procedures/policies including infection control, safety, and quality improvements.

Skills:

1. Skill in helping patients develop or recover reliable communication and swallowing so they can fulfill their educational, vocational, and social roles.

2. Skill in working with family members to recognize and change behavior patterns that impede communication and treatment and show them communication-enhancing techniques to use at home.

3. Skill in collaborating with other clinicians including physicians, social workers, psychologists, and other therapists to develop/implement treatment plans for patients.

Abilities:

1. Ability to effectively communicate diagnostic tests results, diagnoses, and proposed treatment in a manner easily understood by their patients and their families.

2. Ability to approach problems and analyze test results objectively.

3. Ability to be supportive, patient, and compassionate and have good listening skills.

Equipment Operated: Standard office equipment including computer hardware and software. Some specialized speech-language instruments.

Work Environment: Variety of office and exam room settings. Some exposure to bodily fluids and to conditions common to a clinic setting.

Mental/Physical Requirements: Combination of sitting, standing, and walking. Occasionally may need to help with patient transfer/transport. May need to lift/carry up to 30 pounds. Some stress related to dealing with complex cases.

Surgical/Operating Technologist

Job Title:	Surgical/Operating Technologist
Department:	Surgical
Immediate Supervisor Title:	Operating Room Supervisor
Job Supervisory Responsibilities:	None
General Summary:	This nonexempt position is responsible for assisting in surgical operations as part of a team under the supervision of surgeons, registered nurses, or other surgical personnel.

Essential Job Responsibilities:

1. Helps prepare the operating room by setting up surgical instruments and equipment, sterile drapes, and sterile solutions.
2. Assembles both sterile and nonsterile equipment, as well as adjusts and checks it to ensure it is working properly.
3. Prepares patients for surgery by washing, shaving, and disinfecting incision sites.
4. Transports patients to the operating room, helps position them on the operating table, and covers them with sterile surgical drapes. Checks patient charts. Assists the surgical team with putting on sterile gowns and gloves.
5. Passes instruments and other sterile supplies to surgeons and surgeon assistants during surgery. May hold retractors, cut sutures, and help count sponges, needles, supplies, and instruments. Observes patient vital signs. Helps prepare, care for, and dispose of specimens taken for laboratory analysis and helps apply dressings. May operate sterilizers, lights, or suction machines and helps operate diagnostic equipment.
6. Occasionally helps transfer patients to the recovery room after surgery and cleans/restocks the operating room.

Education:	High school diploma. Surgical technologist training from community/junior colleges, vocational schools, hospitals, or the military.
Experience:	Minimum one year of experience in multispecialty surgical unit, preferably in clinic setting.
Other Requirements:	Technologists may obtain voluntary professional certification from the Liaison Council on Certification for the Surgical Technologist by graduating from one of its accredited programs and passing a national certification exam. Continuing education or reexamination is required to maintain certification every four years.

Performance Requirements: *Knowledge:*

1. Knowledge of biology, chemistry, and mathematics.
2. Knowledge of anatomy, physiology, microbiology, pharmacology, professional ethics, and medical terminology.
3. Knowledge of safety, infection control, and quality improvement protocols.

Skills:

1. Skill in operating surgical equipment including both sterile and nonsterile equipment.
2. Skill in staying abreast of new developments.
3. Skill in maintaining sterile environment.

Abilities:

1. Ability to respond quickly in order to have instruments and other sterile supplies ready for surgeons without being told.
2. Ability to remain emotionally stable, conscientious, and orderly to handle the demands of the operating room environment.
3. Ability to demonstrate eye–hand coordination, manual/finger dexterity, and agility.

Equipment Operated: Variety of surgical equipment and instruments including sterilizers, lights, suction machines, and diagnostic equipment.

Work Environment: Primarily operating room setting. Frequent contact with diverse individuals. Maximum exposure to infection, bodily fluids, and sharp instruments. May be exposed to communicable diseases and unpleasant sights, odors, and materials.

Mental/Physical Requirements: Variety of standing, walking, bending, stooping, twisting, and reaching. Requires occasional lifting/carrying/moving of equipment and supplies up to 50 pounds. Frequent stress from surgical life-and-death responsibilities. Must stand for long periods and remain alert during operations.

Volunteer Coordinator

Job Title:	Volunteer Coordinator
Department:	Clinical Services
Immediate Supervisor Title:	Clinical Services Manager
Job Supervisory Responsibilities:	None

General Summary: An exempt position responsible for planning and directing a volunteer program to assist with medical practice activities, which may range from being greeters to helping seniors identify community resources.

Essential Job Responsibilities:

1. Manages volunteer program, including planning, policy making, recruiting, matching, evaluating, and recognizing volunteers. Assesses medical practice needs and compares with volunteer skills, matching compatible individuals with appropriate departments.

2. Develops and implements a recruiting plan to attract specific kinds of volunteers; conducts interviews and reference checks; arranges for candidates to meet with staff managers seeking volunteers to ensure match; participates in selection decisions; ensures appropriate orientation to medical practice policies including customer service, confidentiality, infection control, and safety protocols; provides ongoing training and oversight ensuring appropriate supervision and utilization of volunteers.

3. Institutes a computerized record-keeping system for tracking volunteer efforts including time records. Compiles data, evaluates results, and reports outcomes to highlight value of volunteer program to organization.

4. Plans regular informal recognition activities for volunteers and an annual formal recognition event attended by key staff.

5. Collaborates with community volunteer resource agencies on promoting volunteer opportunities and providing training on volunteer management topics.

Education: Bachelor's degree required, preferably in health field or social services.

Experience: Minimum three years of volunteer management experience, preferably in health care or human services organization.

Other Requirements: Continuing education by taking ongoing volunteer management courses.

Performance Requirements: *Knowledge:*

1. Knowledge of volunteer management principles and practices from recruiting to recognition.

2. Knowledge of medical practice services and of departments that could benefit from volunteer assistance.

3. Knowledge of community resources related to volunteer management.

Skills:

1. Skill in recruiting potential candidates and matching to medical practice needs via a variety of marketing techniques including making presentations.

2. Skill in establishing systems to train and manage volunteers.

3. Skill in ensuring volunteer recognition for their contributions.

Abilities:

1. Ability to interview potential volunteers effectively and identify those who will fit into the medical practice culture well.

2. Ability to motivate volunteers to contribute time and effort to the medical practice.

3. Ability to promote volunteer assistance to medical practice department managers.

Equipment Operated: Standard office equipment particularly computer hardware and software programs applicable to volunteer management. Occasional use of audiovisual equipment for training and presentations.

Work Environment: Combination of medical office rooms and community resource centers. Good lighting and ventilation. Controlled exposure to patients.

Mental/Physical Requirements: Variety of walking, sitting, standing. Occasionally lifts/carries/moves equipment weighing up to 50 pounds. Low level of stress.

About the Authors

Courtney Price, PhD, specializes in the human resource (HR) management needs of medical practices. She is the author of the original edition of *The Group Practice Personnel Policies Manual,* a series of *MGMA HR Issues* (formerly *Personnel Postscript)* – a quarterly newsletter for HR professionals co-authored with Bruce Stickler, JD. In addition, she has written a series of human resource management books for MGMA. Price is a professional speaker specializing in innovation, technology commercialization, and entrepreneurship. She has written more than 14 books on these topics for John Wiley & Sons, McGraw-Hill, and other publishers. She founded the Entrepreneurial Education Foundation in 1994 and co-founded Premier FastTrac™ in 1996, the leading business training and development program for entrepreneurs. Price is currently president of VentureQuest Ltd., a management consulting and training firm that helps organizations introduce new products and services while increasing revenues by capitalizing on the development of people, technologies, and market opportunities. She became the first Scholar-in-Residence at The Kauffman Center for Entrepreneurial Leadership and serves as a visiting professor at major universities around the world.

Alys Novak, MBA, is president of Discovery Communications, Inc., a publishing and consulting/training firm. Her many assignments in the health care field have focused on medical practices, home health, and rural health. Her fields of expertise include strategic planning, marketing, performance management, and compensation. For many years she served as adjunct faculty at Metropolitan State College of Denver and the University of Colorado, teaching a variety of business topics. She has co-authored several books, including *User-Friendly Psychology for Medical Practices* and *Financial Management for Nonprofits.* She is also the author of *Governing Policies for Medical Practices.* Novak co-authored *The Medical Practice Performance Management Manual* and the *HR Policies & Procedures Manual for Medical Practices,* fourth edition, with Courtney Price. For more than two decades, she has edited publications for MGMA on a variety of topics. Until recently, she served as a project manager for the Visiting Nurse Corporation of Colorado, Inc., specializing in quality assurance, patient satisfaction, volunteer resources, marketing, and business planning.

APPENDIX: Additional HR Management Resources Available from MGMA

HR Policies & Procedures

Courtney Price, PhD, DPA, and Alys Novak, MBA

Best seller!
Includes disk of
HR policies

Covering the most pressing HR events this comprehensive manual helps practice managers set procedures and policies for managing staff and allocating resources, while it also gives tips on developing an employee handbook.

2007, 400 pp., ISBN: 978-1-56829-278-6

Item 6634
Nonmember: $211
Affiliate: $162
Member: $135

Human Resource Management Assessment CD
Core Learning Series Level 2

Part of the American College of Medical Practice Executives (ACMPE) professional development assessments series, this assessment is designed to test your knowledge of topics such as employee appraisal and evaluation systems, conflict resolution programs, and compliance with employment law. (ACMPE is the certification and standard-setting body of MGMA.)

- Identify core strengths and areas for improvement
- Receive 2.0 credit hours as assigned by ACMPE
- View questions along with correct answers
- Receive immediate results on completion
- Gain clear direction on where to focus your development

Item 6678
Nonmember: $99
Affiliate: $99
Member: $99
MGMA and ACMPE Member: $75
ACMPE member: $75

277

Medical Practice Management Body of Knowledge Review: Human Resource Management
Core Learning Series Level 1

Grasp the foundational knowledge on human resources of a medical practice with this book –
part of the *Medical Practice Management Body of Knowledge Review Series.* It provides a review of the
basic skills needed in medical practice, specifically focusing on the staffing and other human-resource
issues of the practice and highlighting key concepts, tasks, terminology, regulations, and key resources.

Buy the set
and get the
Overview booklet
and the
Knowledge Assessment
on CD (worth $166)
for free!

Item 6357
Nonmember: $47
Affiliate: $36
Member: $30
MGMA and ACMPE Member: $27

Item 6494 – boxed set of eight
Nonmember: $376
Affiliate: $288
Member: $240
MGMA and ACMPE Member: $216

Tasks Covered

- Task 1 – Develop compensation and benefits programs consistent with the values of the organization
- Task 2 – Establish job classification systems
- Task 3 – Develop employee placement programs and facilitate workforce planning
- Task 4 – Establish employee appraisal and evaluation systems
- Task 5 – Develop and implement employee training programs
- Task 6 – Establish employee relations and conflict resolution programs
- Task 7 – Maintain compliance with employment laws

Medical Practice Performance Management Manual: How to Evaluate Employees, 2nd edition

Courtney Price, PhD, DPA, and Alys Novak, MBA

Includes forms
and checklists!

Managers must know the current trends in performance management. Learn how to maximize today's
technology to provide critical performance data and gives ideas on classic performance triggers such as
compensation, self-management, flexibility, and goal-setting. Includes forms, checklists and other tools
to help you find the right techniques to enhance your employees' performance.

2001, 188 pp., ISBN: 1-56829-148-5

Item 5820
Nonmember: $46
Affiliate: $35
Member: $29 – was $55

Physician Compensation Plans: State-of-the-Art Strategies
Core Learning Series Level 2

Bruce A. Johnson, JD, MPA, and Deborah L. Walker Keegan, PhD, FACMPE

Navigate the maze of methods by which income for physicians is determined and paid in a wide variety of health care organizations, including group practices, academic medical centers, hospitals, and integrated delivery systems. Get innovative approaches to physician compensation. This book covers:

- Plan development and information on pay-for-performance programs
- Implementation methods
- Legal and regulatory compliance issues
- Pros and cons of various plans
- Methods to achieve physician buy-in

This is your step-by-step guide to creating a beneficial compensation plan for all parties. It shows you "how to get from here to there" and covers all the bases.

2006, 566 pp., ISBN: 1-56829-275-9

Item 6451
Nonmember: $209
Affiliate: $159
Member: $129
MGMA and ACMPE Member: $ 116.10

"I have yet to see a text that so thoroughly covers the complicated subject of physician compensation as this one. The authors are very well-known for their expertise, and I believe the combination of Walker and Johnson has produced a resource that is beyond compare."

Chuck Moses, FACMPE
Chief Administrative Officer
Wyoming Brain and Spine Associates, Casper, Wyo.

Best-seller!

Rightsizing: Appropriate Staffing for Your Medical Practice
Core Learning Series Level 2

Deborah Walker, MBA, FACMPE, and David N. Gans, MSHA, FACMPE

Rightsize your practice for the right number and mix of staff to ensure optimal physician productivity, practice efficiency, and financial performance. Find a systematic approach to rightsizing with the five-step process to realign staffing levels and responsibilities. You'll find the comprehensive data tables, practice models, and a staffing resource allocation tool very useful.

2003, 178 pp., ISBN 1-56829-149-3

Item 5692
Nonmember: $125
Affiliate: $96
Member: $80
MGMA and ACMPE Member: $72

Rx for Business Success: Joining a Medical Practice

Learn the pros and cons of joining a medical practice. Covering practice entities, structures, locations, and malpractice and employment laws, this book can help practice managers and physicians make sound decisions about joining a group practice. Also, use this booklet to understand the differences between a group practice setting and a hospital setting.

Item 6340
Nonmember: $39
Affiliate: $30
Member: $25

Rx for Business Success: Joining a Medical Practice DVD and book package

Physicians need more than good clinical skills for a successful practice. That includes knowing how the entire billing and collection cycle works – from the time a patient calls for his or her first appointment to when you receive payment for the visit. Key to this process is using accurate coding so that you are paid appropriately for your services. Gain these important insights and more with the *Rx for Business Success* DVD and book, which features self-paced Webcasts.

The DVD covers:

- Coding systems: How they affect reimbursement and your pay
- Setting fee schedules: Submitting claims, handling denied claims, and managing accounts receivable
- Business practices that ensure legal and regulatory compliance
- Safeguarding your medical practice from fraud and embezzlement
- Several practical downloadable tools, such as contracting essentials, a claim-filing checklist, a sample explanation of benefits, and a glossary of managed-care terms

Get an overview of the most important aspects of practice operations and management with this package.

Item RXBUS
Nonmember: $199
Member: $179

What they never taught us in medical school

"Physicians today have mastered the clinical skills necessary to provide high-quality care to their patients, but most have not had an opportunity to learn even the basics of the 'business of medicine.' This book is designed to introduce young physicians to what they need to know in order to make informed career decisions about their medical practice. While it is not a comprehensive medical practice management textbook, it is a useful primer on the most important aspects of practice operations and management."

William F. Jessee, MD, FACMPE
President and CEO
Medical Group Management Association, Englewood, Colo.

WEBCASTS AND AUDIO CONFERENCES

Here Today, Here Tomorrow: Transforming Your Workforce from High Turnover to High Retention

Please note: Continuing education credit is not granted for listening to tapes, CDs, or on-demand Webcasts.

Recorded by Gregory P. Smith, MS

This recorded presentation will enable you to:

- Identify the factors leading to turnover.
- Apply a five-step process to create a work environment that attracts, keeps, and motivates staff.

Recorded on 3/23/06

Item 6549 - Tape	Item 6550 - CD	Item 6551 - On-demand Webcast
Nonmember: $231.50	Nonmember: $241.50	Nonmember: $239
Affiliate: $181.50	Affiliate: $191.50	Affiliate: $189
Member: $171.50	Member: $181.50	Member: $179

Leading the Parade: The Administrator's Role in Service Quality Leadership

Recorded by Vicky Bradford, PhD

This recorded presentation will enable you to:

- Recognize what being "passionate about service" means and how to explain it to others.
- Recognize the range of choices for seeking service feedback.
- Determine the methods for motivating staff and transforming them into service champions.

Recorded on 4/13/2006

Item 6552 - Tape	Item 6553 - CD	Item 6554 - On-demand Webcast
Nonmember: $231.50	Nonmember: $241.50	Nonmember: $239
Affiliate: $181.50	Affiliate: $191.50	Affiliate: $189
Member: $171.50	Member: $181.50	Member: $179

INFORMATION EXCHANGES

Information Exchanges are compilations of results from informal questionnaires sent to MGMA members. Information Exchanges show you how others deal with practice management issues, allow you to find colleagues for networking and provide examples of practice documents.

Administrator Incentive Plans

Includes: Eight administrators' incentive plans and key findings
  • Ever wondered what types of incentives other administrators are receiving – and how often?
  • Learn what incentives are most popular among your MGMA peers' practices as well as the average administrator's bonus over the past three years.

2006, 66 pp.

Item 6530
Nonmember: $120
Affiliate: $60
Member: $40

Administrator Performance Appraisals

Includes: 13 sample performance appraisals and key findings

  • Do you like your current performance appraisal system?
  • Get new ideas from your MGMA peers on how to enhance the process to measure your performance.

2004, 97 pp.

Item 4027
Nonmember: $120
Affiliate: $60
Member: $35

Alternative Medicine Providers – Employ, Contract or Refer

Includes: Sample of a contract for an alternative medicine provider and key findings

  • Are you losing potential revenue by not offering patients alternative medicine options?
  • Find out how your MGMA peers have integrated complementary and alternative medicine into their practices.
  • Find out the types of providers used, how they are reimbursed and compensation differences.

2005, 13 pp.

Item 5050
Nonmember: $90
Affiliate: $50
Member: $25

Buy-In and Buy-Out Agreements

Includes: Four sample agreements and key findings

- How do your peers handle buy-in and buy-out agreements with new docs?
- How long before the physician is allowed to buy in and how much does it cost?
- Find out how your MGMA peers give new physicians an option to purchase shares in the practice partnership or corporation.
- Get ideas on creating an appropriate agreement.

2006, 81 pp.

Item 6529
Nonmember: $120
Affiliate: $60
Member: $35

Employee Attitude Survey

Includes: 11 sample employee attitude surveys and a statistical summary report

- Is your staff happy? Find out for sure with satisfaction surveys.
- Your MGMA peers share how often they conduct surveys, who sees the results and how those results are put to use in the practice.

2003, 53 pp.

Item 4569
Nonmember: $103
Affiliate: $54
Member: $36

Employee Benefits

Includes: 15 sample employee benefit policies or procedures and key findings

- Ever wondered what types of benefits your peers are offering to their nonphysician staff and employees?
- What's the dollar amount employees can use on continuing education? And what percent does the practice contribute to employee pension/retirement plans?
- Find out how many days of vacation leave and sick time, per year, are offered to employees, and how those are tiered based on years of service.

2006, 128 pp.

Item 4798
Nonmember: $163
Affiliate: $85
Member: $55

Employee Incentive Plans

Includes: Five sample employee incentive plans and key findings

- What types of incentives are used for medical office employees (not including physicians and administrators)?
- Find out how often your MGMA member peers' distribute employee incentives, which employees are included in the incentive plan, and how the incentive plan helps employees in their work environment.
- Find out who developed the practice's employee incentive plan and as a percentage of base pay/ salary, what the average bonus was over the past three years.

2006, 43 pp.

Item 6567
Nonmember: $90
Affiliate: $50
Member: $25

Employee Performance Appraisals

Includes: 49 sample appraisal forms and key findings

- Whether you use employee performance evaluations or are only considering them, you can glean useful ideas from your MGMA peers.
- See the details of your colleagues' evaluation procedures, including how often evaluations are done, who conducts the appraisal, and whether the process produces after-the-fact satisfactory results.

2005, 264 pp.

Item 4237
Nonmember: $145
Affiliate: $70
Member: $45

Group Practice Administrator — Employment Contracts

Includes: Seven copies of employment contracts and compensation/incentive plans, as well as a summary of the questionnaire results

- Is it time to review your compensation plan and employment contract?
- Learn the methods and formulas your MGMA peers are using and what clauses are included in their contracts.

2004, 65 pp.

Item 4455
Nonmember: $103
Affiliate: $54
Member: $33

Group Practice Administrator — Job Descriptions

Includes: 56 job descriptions and a statistical summary of questionnaire responses

- Do you want to know what responsibilities your MGMA peers are handling?
- Discover how to accurately communicate your duties and responsibilities to your board.
- See which major duties administrators are most often assigned.
- Learn who updates written job descriptions and how often updates should occur.

2003, 257 pp.

Item 3933
Nonmember: $163
Affiliate: $84
Member: $52

Health Care Recruiting Firms

Includes: A contract description and key findings

- Is it advantageous to use the services of an executive/health care recruitment firm?
- Find out which of your MGMA member peers used a firm to fill positions, what services were provided, the name of the firms, and the price range paid for a successful placement.
- Discover if the practices have a standing engagement or retainer with a recruiting firm.

2005, 29 pp.

Item 6523
Nonmember: $90
Affiliate: $50
Member: $25

Income Distribution – Call Coverage

Includes: One compensation plan and a statistical summary of questionnaire responses

- Are you having problems distributing call coverage among physicians?
- Find out how your MGMA peers use compensation to manage this task.
- Understand what call coverage is really worth (per-hour or per-call).
- See if other groups pay physicians for each shift or for weekend calls only.

2002, 41 pp.

Item 5384
Nonmember: $88
Affiliate: $45
Member: $28

Income Distribution – Expense Allocation

Includes: 18 sample income-distribution and expense-allocation plans, a statistical summary of questionnaire responses, and an analysis

- Could a charge-back system improve or reduce your practice overhead?
- See how the strategy works for your MGMA peers as they note which expenses they include in their income distribution formula.
- Find out how the system affects productivity and overhead.

2003, 117 pp.

Item 4294
Nonmember: $145
Affiliate: $77
Member: $50

Income Distribution – Incentive Plans

Includes: Seven samples of income-distribution plans and a statistical summary of questionnaire responses

- Are you looking for new methods to increase your physicians' productivity?
- See how your MGMA peers use a variety of incentive-based income distribution plans to help them meet this primary goal.

2004, 55 pp.

Item 4890
Nonmember: $100
Affiliate: $50
Member: $30

Income Distribution Plans – Physicians

Includes: Eight sample income distribution plans and key findings

- Is your physician income distribution appropriate for your practice?
- Get a new perspective from your MGMA peers – learn the plans that work for them.
- Find out how they measure physicians' satisfaction.

2006, 54 pp.

Item 6632
Nonmember: $90
Affiliate: $50
Member: $25

Medical Directors / Managing Partners Duties and Compensation Methods

Includes: Seven sample medical director/managing partner's job descriptions or employment contracts and key findings

- Do you wonder if you're asking too much or too little of a physician who serves as your medical director or physician administrator?
- What are their major responsibilities, how many hours do they work in this capacity, and how are they compensated for managing these duties? Compensation methods for these duties are included, as well as hourly compensation for these duties.
- Use the sample job descriptions to manage this position.

2006, 62 pp.

Item 6601
Nonmember: $120
Affiliate: $60
Member: $35

Medical Directors – Hospital / Health Facilities

Includes: Two examples of medical directors' contracts and a statistical summary of questionnaire responses

- Is your practice contracting with a hospital? Do you need information on how to structure the arrangement?
- Learn how your MGMA peers' physicians typically handle medical director responsibilities in a hospital or other health care setting and how they are compensated.

2003, 37 pp.

Item 5414
Nonmember: $80
Affiliate: $41
Member: $26

Nonphysician Provider Employment Contracts and Compensation Plans

Includes: 12 copies of nonphysician provider compensation plans and key findings

- What is the best way to compensate your nonphysician providers?
- How much do you pay your physicians to supervise the nonphysician providers?
- Learn if your MGMA peers offer straight salaries, incentive plans, or pay based on production. (Salary figures are not provided.)

2005, 103 pp.

Item 5051
Nonmember: $145
Affiliate: $70
Member: $45

Nonphysician Provider Performance Appraisals

Includes: 10 sample appraisals and key findings

- Are you satisfied with your mid-level nonphysician providers?
- Do you have a mechanism in place to review these employees?
- Glean useful ideas from your MGMA peers on how reviews are conducted and if it's beneficial to the group.

2005, 77 pp.

Item 6323
Nonmember: $120
Affiliate: $60
Member: $35

Physician and Nonphysician Provider's Job Descriptions

Includes: Two physician and 11 nonphysician job descriptions and key findings

- Is there confusion about how duties and protocols are divided among your group's providers (physicians, physician assistants, nurse practitioners, etc.)?
- Use these sample job descriptions to help define the parameters of your providers' responsibilities.

2004, 77 pp.

Item 4576
Nonmember: $120
Affiliate: $60
Member: $35

Physicians – Benefits

Includes: 18 copies of physician benefit descriptions, a statistical summary of questionnaire responses, and an analysis

- Do your physicians receive the same retirement benefits as their peers?
- Find out what benefits your MGMA member peers' practices offer their physicians.
- Learn the most common types of pension/retirement plans, as well as the average leave time allowed for continuing medical education.

2003, 162 pp.

Item 3538
Nonmember: $153
Affiliate: $79
Member: $52

Physicians – Discipline

Includes: Seven sample policies, a statistical summary of questionnaire responses, and an analysis

- Have you ever met a physician who was inappropriate or abusive?
- Be prepared by reviewing the disciplinary procedures used by your MGMA peers.

2003, 91 pp.

Item 3091
Nonmember: $130
Affiliate: $69
Member: $43

Physician Employment Contracts

Includes: 11 copies of physician employment contracts and a statistical summary of questionnaire responses

- Are you looking to hire a new physician or review existing physician employment contracts?
- Find out the clauses your MGMA peers use in their physician employment contracts, including compensation methods, productivity measures, and noncompete clauses.

2004, 115 pp.

Item 4990
Nonmember: $140
Affiliate: $70
Member: $45

Physicians – Extended Leave Policies

Includes: A sample extended leave policy and key findings

- Has one of your physicians ever taken an extended leave (6+ weeks)? Was the process outlined in practice bylaws or in the physician's contract?
- See how your MGMA member peers handle their patient load while accommodating a physician on extended leave.
- Learn how the practice covers the physician's expenses and benefits, under what circumstances they are allowed extended leave, and who is eligible for extended leave benefits (excluding FMLA).
- Find out how much advance notice (in weeks) is required for physicians wishing to take leave and the minimum/maximum (in weeks) allowed.

2006, 55 pp.

Item 6651
Nonmember: $90
Affiliate: $50
Member: $25

Physicians – Locum Tenens

Includes: A sample independent contractor's agreement and key findings

- Under what circumstances would you need to contract with a locum tenen?
- Find out how your MGMA member peers' practices bill for the locum's service as well as how the locum is compensated, including exactly what the locum is reimbursed for and the average hourly rate paid for the locum.
- Learn how the practice located the locum and if the practice notifies the patients of the locum's presence.

2006, 31 pp.

Item 3475
Nonmember: $90
Affiliate: $50
Member: $25

Physicians – Part-Time or Partially Retired

Includes: Two sample employment contracts and written policies for part-time physicians

- Do you know how to set fair compensation guidelines for your part-time or partially retired physicians?
- Benefit from your MGMA member peers' experience by reading how they share call and distribute income to this class of physicians.
- See how income can be reduced for not taking call coverage/hospital rounds, and note benefits and malpractice policies for these doctors.

2006, 31 pp.

Item 6566
Nonmember: $90
Affiliate: $50
Member: $25

Physician Performance Appraisal

Includes: Six appraisal/performance forms and a statistical summary of questionnaire responses with an analysis

- Need to implement a new physician performance-management process?
- Find out how your MGMA peers conduct and measure physician performance reviews and whether the evaluations affect physician compensation.

2003, 74 pp.

Item 4810
Nonmember: $115
Affiliate: $60
Member: $40

Physicians – Retirement and Succession Planning

Includes: Three samples letters of retirement notification letters or correspondence (to patients, third-party payers, media, referring physicians) and key findings

- Are you worried about a physician's impending retirement?
- Find out how your MGMA member peers handled retirement planning for their doctors, how physicians are allowed to phase out of their duties and patient load, and how the patients were distributed in the practice.
- Discover the average age of the retiring physicians (it's not 65!) and how much advance notice is usually required for a physician wishing to retire.

2006, 29 pp.

Item 6600
Nonmember: $90
Affiliate: $50
Member: $25

Physician Satisfaction Survey

Includes: 15 sample physician satisfaction questionnaires, a statistical summary of questionnaire responses, and an analysis

- Are you concerned with physician turnover rates?
- Nip the problem in the bud by creating a physician satisfaction survey/feedback tool.
- Find out how often your MGMA member peers query their physicians as well as referring physicians and how they use the results.

2003, 68 pp.

Item 4750
Nonmember: $108
Affiliate: $59
Member: $38

Physicians – Service Guidelines and Code of Conduct

Includes: Four sample practice clinical service guidelines and/or "codes of conduct" and key findings

- We all know about the Hippocratic Oath, but what about a Practice "Code of Conduct" for physician behavior?
- Learn how your MGMA member peers developed clinical service guidelines and/or a "code of conduct" for physician behavior as it relates to patients, peers, and staff.
- See how the guidelines were developed and introduced to physicians, and how the guidelines have been used to frame disciplinary actions.

2006, 34 pp.

Item 6673
Nonmember: $90
Affiliate: $50
Member: $25

Physicians - Income Distribution – RVUs

Includes: Two sample independent contractor's agreements and key findings

- Has your practice made the transition to using relative value unit-(RVU-)-based income distribution plans?
- Ascertain how to best use RVUs to determine physician compensation.
- Find out if your MGMA member peers use RVUs to determine total compensation, or if it's a percentage of compensation (and if so, which percentage).
- Find out how often the compensation plan is updated and if the physicians can buy in to the methodology of using RVUs in their compensation plans.

2006, 29 pp.

Item 5137
Nonmember: $90
Affiliate: $50
Member: $25

Index

Items in *italic* indicate additional resources.

D

E

F

G

H

I

J

About the CD-ROM

Included with this manual is a CD-ROM containing the text for the generic job descriptions in this book. These can be used as a starting point as you develop or revise your practice's job descriptions. Just pull up a description example and modify it to fit your medical practice. Be sure to have your descriptions reviewed by legal counsel to ensure that they comply with state and federal laws and other legal requirements.

How to Use the Files on Your CD-ROM

The CD-ROM presents the job description examples in Microsoft®Word format. You must have Microsoft®Word installed on your hard drive to use the CD-ROM. To adapt any file to your own practice, simply follow the instructions below. The CD-ROM will work on Windows and Mac platforms.

Microsoft®Word Instructions for Windows

1. Insert the CD in your CD-ROM drive.
2. Double-click on the "My Computer" icon, and then double click on the CD drive icon.
3. Double-click on the folder named "Job Description Manual."
4. The folders you see are organized into the same categories as those in Chapter 5. Double click on the appropriate job description folder, double click on the category folder, and then double click to open the Microsoft®Word job description file.
5. If you have trouble reading the files, click on "View", and then "Normal."
6. To adapt the file, you must save it to your hard drive first, renaming it if you like. After you have resaved it, the file can be edited.